Foreword

Welcome to "Parenting Pearls: The Journey Begins; Building Strong Foundation." In the vast sea of parenting advice and guidance, this book stands out as a precious gem, offering invaluable insights and wisdom to parents embarking on the exhilarating yet challenging journey of raising children.

Parenting is perhaps the most profound and rewarding experience life has to offer. It's a journey filled with moments of joy, laughter, and boundless love, but also one fraught with uncertainty, doubt, and occasional chaos. In this book, you'll find a beacon of light to guide you through the highs and lows, helping you navigate the often turbulent waters of parenthood and confidence.

As parents, we are entrusted with the remarkable responsibility of shaping the future through our children. Every decision we make, every word we speak, and every action we take leaves an indelible imprint on their hearts and minds. This book equips us with the knowledge, tools, and inspiration to nurture our children's growth, cultivate their potential, and instill in them the values and virtues that will guide them throughout their lives.

Drawing upon a wealth of experience, research, and timeless wisdom, this book offers practical advice on a myriad of topics, from fostering healthy attachment and communication to setting boundaries, managing conflicts, and cultivating resilience in our children. But beyond mere techniques and strategies, this book reminds us of the profound importance of presence, empathy, and unconditional love in raising happy, confident, and well-adjusted children.

As you embark on this transformative journey of parenthood, may this book serve as your trusted companion, offering solace in times of uncertainty, inspiration in moments of doubt, and guidance on the path toward building a strong foundation for your family. May it empower you to embrace the challenges, cherish the joys, and savor the precious moments of connection and growth with your children.

Table of Contents

Section 1: The Journey Begins

Chapter 1: Introducing the Journey of Parenthood: The Joys, Challenges, and Transformative Moments

1.1 The Beginning of a Journey

Parenthood is a journey unlike any other. From the moment you learn of the impending arrival of a child, your life begins to shift in profound and unexpected ways. The anticipation, excitement, and nervousness mingle together, creating a whirlwind of emotions. Parenthood marks the onset of an unparalleled voyage. It commences with the revelation of an impending addition to the family, triggering a cascade of transformative experiences. The amalgamation of anticipation, exhilaration, and apprehension sets the stage for a whirlwind of emotions, reshaping one's existence in profound and unforeseen manners.

Parenthood is an odyssey that traverses the depths of human experience, an adventure that transcends the boundaries of time and space. It commences with the whisper of a promise, a flutter of anticipation upon hearing the news of an impending arrival. In that moment, the universe seems to pause, holding its breath as the realization sinks in: life as you know it is about to change forever.

The journey of parenthood is marked by a kaleidoscope of emotions, each more vibrant and intense than the last. Anticipation dances with excitement, casting a spell of euphoria upon expectant parents, while nervousness lurks in the shadows, a constant companion whispering tales of uncertainty and doubt. Together, these emotions weave a tapestry of anticipation, a symphony of feelings that crescendo with the arrival of the little one.

With each passing day, the contours of parenthood begin to take shape, revealing themselves in the subtle nuances of daily life. From the gentle flutter of tiny kicks in the womb to the first cries of a newborn, every moment is imbued with a sense of wonder and awe. Sleepless nights blur into hazy days, as parents navigate the uncharted waters of caring for their little one, learning and growing alongside them with each passing moment.

Yet amidst the chaos and the cacophony of parenthood, there is a profound sense of purpose, a deep-seated knowing that this journey is unlike any other. It is a journey of self-discovery and transformation, of sacrifice and unconditional love. It is a journey that challenges the very essence of who we are, pushing us beyond our limits and shaping us into the parents we were meant to be.

As the days turn into weeks, and the weeks into years, parenthood evolves into a masterpiece of love and devotion. It is a journey that unfolds in the laughter of children and the quiet moments of reflection, in the shared joys and the whispered secrets exchanged in the dead of night. It is a journey that transcends time and space, weaving its way through the fabric of our lives and leaving an indelible mark upon our hearts.

In the end, parenthood is more than just a journey; it is a testament to the resilience of the human spirit, a celebration of the boundless capacity of the human heart to love and to nurture. It is a journey unlike any other, a journey that forever changes us and shapes the very essence of who we are.

1.2 Embracing the Joy of Parenthood

Embracing the joy of parenting entails immersing oneself fully in the myriad experiences that come with raising a child. It's about recognizing that while parenthood is undoubtedly challenging, the rewards it offers are unparalleled. Every day presents an opportunity to witness the marvels of a child's growth and development, from their first tentative steps to the moment they confidently express themselves.

In the midst of hectic schedules and seemingly endless responsibilities, it's essential to pause and savor the small, precious moments that make parenting so fulfilling. These moments can be as simple as a spontaneous hug from your child or sharing a laugh over a silly joke. They serve as gentle reminders of the beauty and innocence that children embody, infusing our lives with warmth and light.

Moreover, embracing the joy of parenting means fostering a deep connection with your child, built on love, trust, and understanding. It involves actively engaging with them, whether through meaningful conversations, imaginative play, or shared activities. By being present and attentive, we create lasting memories and forge bonds that endure a lifetime.

Parenting also provides an opportunity for personal growth and self-discovery. As we navigate the ups and downs of raising a child, we uncover strengths we never knew we possessed and learn valuable lessons about patience, resilience, and empathy. It's a journey of continuous learning and evolution, where every triumph and setback shapes us into more compassionate and capable individuals.

Embracing the joy of parenting is about cherishing the privilege of guiding another human being through life's adventures. It's about finding fulfillment in the simple yet profound moments of connection, love, and shared experiences. Through the laughter, tears, and everything in between, parenthood offers a profound sense of purpose and meaning that enriches our lives in ways we could never have imagined.

1.3 Facing the Challenges Head-On

Facing the challenges of parenting head-on requires a blend of resilience, empathy, and practical strategies. It's about acknowledging that parenthood, while incredibly rewarding, also comes with its fair share of trials and tribulations. Sleepless nights, tantrums, and tears are just some of the obstacles that parents encounter along the journey of raising a child.

First and foremost, it's crucial to approach these challenges with honesty and compassion. Parenthood isn't always picture-perfect, and it's okay to admit when things are tough. By normalizing the struggles of parenting, we create a supportive environment where parents feel understood and validated in their experiences.

One of the key aspects of facing parenting challenges head-on is exploring the feelings of frustration and doubt that inevitably arise. Whether it's grappling with a defiant toddler or navigating the complexities of teenage angst, it's natural to question our abilities as parents. By acknowledging these feelings without judgment, we open the door to growth and resilience.

Practical strategies play a vital role in overcoming parenting challenges. From setting clear boundaries and establishing routines to practicing self-care and seeking support from loved ones, there are countless ways to navigate difficult moments and resilience. By equipping parents with tangible tools and resources, we empower them to tackle challenges proactively and confidently.

Facing parenting challenges head-on involves fostering open communication within the family unit. Encouraging honest dialogue allows parents and children to express their thoughts, feelings, and concerns in a safe and supportive environment. By listening actively and empathizing with one another, families can work together to find effective solutions to the challenges they face.

Facing the challenges of parenting head-on is about embracing the journey in its entirety—the ups, the downs, and everything in between. It's about recognizing that growth often emerges from adversity and that every challenge presents an opportunity for learning and transformation. By approaching parenting with resilience, compassion, and practicality, we can navigate even the most daunting obstacles.

1.4 Embracing Transformative Moments

Embracing transformative moments as a parent involves recognizing the profound impact that parenthood has on our lives and embracing the growth and self-discovery that come with the journey. Parenthood has a unique ability to challenge us, pushing us beyond our comfort zones and prompting deep reflection on who we are and who we aspire to be.

One of the most transformative aspects of parenthood is learning to let go of perfectionism. As parents, we often enter this role with high expectations for ourselves and our children. However, we quickly learn that perfection is an unrealistic standard and that embracing the beauty of imperfection is far more fulfilling. Through the messy, unpredictable moments of parenting, we discover the beauty in the imperfect and learn to celebrate the journey rather than fixating on the destination.

Parenthood also teaches us valuable lessons about love, patience, and resilience. The unconditional love we feel for our children transcends boundaries and reshapes our understanding of what it means to care for another human being. It challenges us to cultivate patience in the face of adversity and to persevere even when the road ahead seems daunting. In moments of uncertainty and doubt, parenthood calls upon us to dig deep and find the strength to keep moving forward.

Parenthood shapes our identity in profound ways, challenging us to redefine our priorities and values. It prompts us to confront our strengths and weaknesses, pushing us to become the best versions of ourselves for the sake of our children. Through the highs and lows of parenting, we discover parts of ourselves we never knew existed and develop a newfound sense of purpose and resilience.

Embracing transformative moments as a parent means embracing the journey in its entirety—the moments of joy, the challenges, and everything in between. It's about recognizing that parenthood is not just about raising children but also about nurturing our own growth and development along the way. By embracing the transformative power of parenthood, we can unlock new depths of understanding, compassion, and resilience within ourselves, ultimately becoming better parents and better human beings in the process.

1.5 Finding Balance in Parenthood

Finding balance in parenthood is akin to performing a delicate dance, requiring mindfulness, adaptability, and a willingness to prioritize what truly matters. The myriad roles and responsibilities that come with raising children—from nurturing their growth to managing household tasks—can often feel overwhelming, leaving parents grappling with the challenge of striking a harmonious balance.

Central to achieving balance in parenthood is recognizing the importance of harmonizing the various aspects of life, including work, family, self-care, and relationships. Juggling these competing demands requires intentional effort and a commitment to setting boundaries and priorities. By identifying what truly matters and allocating time and energy accordingly, parents can create a more harmonious and fulfilling life for themselves and their families.

Practical tips for finding balance amidst the chaos of parenthood abound. These may include establishing routines and schedules to create a sense of structure and predictability, delegating tasks and responsibilities to share the workload, and practicing effective time management techniques to make the most of limited resources. Additionally, prioritizing self-care and nurturing relationships can help replenish energy and foster emotional well-being, ultimately enabling parents to better meet the needs of their children.

Finding balance in parenthood requires a willingness to adapt and recalibrate as circumstances change. Flexibility is key as parents navigate the ever-evolving demands of raising children, adjusting their priorities and strategies as needed to maintain equilibrium in the face of new challenges and opportunities.

Finding balance in parenthood is an ongoing process of self-discovery and adjustment, guided by a commitment to nurturing both oneself and one's family. By prioritizing what truly matters and cultivating flexibility and resilience, parents can navigate the complexities of parenthood with greater ease, ultimately fostering a more harmonious and fulfilling family life.

1.6 Cultivating Connection and Bonding

Cultivating connection and bonding between parent and child is at the heart of nurturing a strong and enduring relationship—one that serves as a foundation for emotional well-being and growth. The bond between parent and child is a profound and sacred tie, characterized by love, trust, and mutual understanding.

Central to cultivating this bond is the importance of nurturing secure attachments from infancy onwards. Secure attachment forms the basis of a child's emotional development, providing them with a sense of safety and security that allows them to explore the world with confidence. Parents can foster secure attachments by responding promptly and sensitively to their child's needs, offering comfort and reassurance in times of distress, and consistently providing a nurturing and supportive environment.

Open communication and trust are also essential components of a strong parent-child bond. Creating a safe and non-judgmental space for dialogue allows children to express their thoughts, feelings, and concerns openly, fostering a sense of connection and understanding. By actively listening to their child's perspectives and validating their experiences, parents can strengthen the bond of trust and lay the groundwork for healthy communication and problem-solving skills.

Practical strategies for strengthening the parent-child bond abound. These may include engaging in shared activities and hobbies that foster a sense of closeness and connection, such as reading together, playing games, or exploring nature. Making time for one-on-one interactions, free from distractions, allows parents and children to deepen their connection and create lasting memories together.

The power of presence cannot be overstated in cultivating a strong parent-child bond. Being fully present and engaged in the moment communicates to children that they are valued and cherished, fostering feelings of security and belonging. Even amidst the busyness of daily life, carving out dedicated time for meaningful interactions with our children sends a powerful message of love and prioritizes the bond that binds us together.

Cultivating connection and bonding between parent and child is an ongoing journey that requires intentionality, patience, and unconditional love. By nurturing secure attachments, fostering open communication and trust, and prioritizing meaningful interactions, parents can strengthen the bond with their children and lay the groundwork for a lifetime of love and connection.

1.7 Embracing the Unexpected

Embracing the unexpected as a parent is an essential aspect of navigating the unpredictable journey of parenthood. Parenthood is a rollercoaster ride filled with surprises—some delightful, others daunting—but each contributing to the rich tapestry of experiences that shape our lives and relationships.

One of the most profound lessons parenthood teaches us is to embrace the unexpected twists and turns that come our way. From unexpected challenges like health issues or developmental hurdles to moments of serendipity and joy that catch us off guard, parenthood invites us to surrender our need for control and embrace the beauty of the unknown.

The unpredictable nature of parenting can be both exhilarating and daunting. It challenges us to adapt and grow, pushing us beyond our comfort zones and prompting us to discover reservoirs of strength and resilience we never knew we had. By embracing the unexpected with an open heart and mind, we unlock new depths of understanding and compassion, both for ourselves and for our children.

Embracing the unexpected in parenthood allows us to let go of rigid expectations and embrace the journey as it unfolds. It invites us to release the illusion of control and instead cultivate a sense of curiosity and wonder towards the unknown. In doing so, we open ourselves up to new possibilities and opportunities for growth, both as individuals and as a family.

The beauty of embracing the unexpected lies in the moments of surprise and spontaneity that infuse our lives with joy and meaning. Whether it's witnessing our child's first steps, sharing in their laughter, or finding strength and resilience in the face of adversity, these unexpected moments remind us of the magic and wonder of parenthood.

Embracing the unexpected as a parent is about surrendering to the inherent unpredictability of life and finding beauty and meaning in the journey itself. By letting go of control and embracing the unknown with an open heart and mind, we can navigate the highs and lows of parenthood with greater ease and appreciation, ultimately enriching our lives and deepening our connections with our children.

1.8 Navigating Parenting Styles

Navigating parenting styles is a deeply personal journey, influenced by a myriad of factors including our own upbringing, cultural background, and individual beliefs and values. Every parent brings their own unique perspective to the task of raising children, resulting in a diverse array of parenting styles and philosophies.

One commonly discussed framework for understanding parenting styles is the authoritative-permissive spectrum. At one end, authoritative parenting is characterized by warmth, responsiveness, and clear expectations. Parents who adopt an authoritative style strive to balance nurturing with firm guidance, providing structure and boundaries while also fostering independence and autonomy in their children. This approach is associated with positive outcomes, including higher levels of self-esteem, academic achievement, and social competence.

On the other hand, permissive parenting tends to be more indulgent and lenient, with few demands placed on children. Permissive parents may prioritize their child's happiness and autonomy above all else, often avoiding confrontation and setting few rules or expectations. While permissive parenting can foster a close and affectionate relationship between parent and child, it may also lead to challenges with discipline and self-regulation.

Somewhere in between these extremes lie other parenting styles, such as authoritarian and uninvolved parenting. Authoritarian parents are characterized by high demands and low responsiveness, prioritizing obedience and discipline over warmth and autonomy. Uninvolved parents, meanwhile, are characterized by low levels of both warmth and control, often disengaged or neglectful in their approach to parenting.

Navigating parenting styles involves recognizing the strengths and weaknesses of each approach and finding a balance that aligns with your values and beliefs. It's about being intentional and mindful in our parenting choices, taking into account the unique needs and temperament of our children while also considering the broader cultural and societal context in which we parent.

The goal of navigating parenting styles is to create a nurturing and supportive environment that promotes the healthy development and well-being of our children. By fostering open communication, setting clear expectations, and providing consistent and loving guidance, parents can create a foundation for their children to thrive and flourish, regardless of the specific parenting style they choose to adopt.

1.9 The Power of Presence

In the hustle and bustle of modern life, the concept of presence in parenting holds immense significance. It's all too easy to become swept up in the demands of work, technology, and various commitments, inadvertently allowing moments with our children to slip away unnoticed. Yet, the power of presence lies in its ability to anchor us in the here and now, allowing us to fully engage with our children and savor the richness of the parent-child relationship.

At its core, presence in parenting involves being fully attentive and engaged with our children in the present moment. It means putting aside distractions and giving our undivided focus to the experiences we share with them, whether it's playing together, sharing a meal, or simply engaging in conversation. By cultivating a sense of mindfulness, we can heighten our awareness of the small, fleeting moments that make up the tapestry of parenthood, allowing us to savor them more fully.

Practicing mindfulness is a powerful tool for fostering presence in parenting. Mindfulness involves paying deliberate attention to the present moment without judgment, allowing us to cultivate a deeper sense of awareness and connection with ourselves and others. By incorporating mindfulness practices into our daily lives, such as meditation, deep breathing exercises, or simply taking a moment to pause and center ourselves, we can enhance our ability to be fully present with our children.

Practical tips for incorporating mindfulness into parenting abound. These may include setting aside dedicated time each day for focused interactions with our children, free from distractions such as phones or other electronic devices. Creating rituals or routines, such as bedtime stories or family meals, can also provide opportunities for meaningful connection and presence. Additionally, practicing active listening and validation when communicating with our children can foster deeper connections and a greater sense of trust and understanding.

The power of presence in parenting lies in its ability to enrich our relationships with our children and cultivate a sense of connection and belonging. By slowing down, being fully present, and savoring the simple joys of parenthood, we can create lasting memories and deepen the bond we share with our children, ultimately fostering a sense of security, love, and well-being that will carry them through life.

1.10 Nurturing Resilience in Children

Nurturing resilience in children is a fundamental aspect of parenting, equipping them with the tools and mindset needed to navigate life's inevitable challenges and setbacks with determination. Resilience is the capacity to bounce back from adversity, to adapt in the face of change, and to emerge stronger and more resilient than before.

Central to fostering resilience in children is the recognition that life is full of ups and downs, and that setbacks are a natural part of the human experience. By teaching our children to view challenges as opportunities for growth rather than insurmountable obstacles, we empower them to develop a resilient mindset—one characterized by optimism, perseverance, and a belief in their own abilities.

Practical strategies for nurturing resilience in children abound. These may include teaching them problem-solving skills, encouraging them to break challenges down into manageable steps, and modeling positive coping mechanisms such as deep breathing, mindfulness, or seeking support from others. By providing children with a toolkit of coping strategies, we help them develop the resilience they need to navigate life's ups and downs with confidence and poise.

Positive parenting plays a crucial role in building resilience in children. By providing a nurturing and supportive environment characterized by warmth, acceptance, and encouragement, parents can foster a sense of security and self-worth in their children. Positive reinforcement and praise for effort rather than outcome can help children develop a growth mindset, fostering resilience and a willingness to persevere in the face of setbacks.

Parents can support their children in developing resilience by fostering a sense of autonomy and independence. Allowing children to make decisions and take healthy risks within safe boundaries teaches them to trust in their own abilities and resilience. By providing guidance and support while also allowing room for mistakes and learning, parents can help their children develop the confidence and inner strength needed to navigate life's challenges.

Nurturing resilience in children is about instilling in them the belief that they have the power to overcome adversity and thrive in the face of challenges. By teaching them to view setbacks as opportunities for growth, providing them with practical coping strategies, and fostering a nurturing and supportive environment, parents can empower their children to embrace life's ups and downs with resilience, courage, and optimism.

1.11 The Gift of Imperfection

The gift of imperfection in parenthood is a profound lesson that reminds us of our shared humanity and the beauty of embracing life's messy, imperfect moments. As parents, we often place immense pressure on ourselves to be perfect—to have all the answers, to never make mistakes, and to provide our children with nothing less than the best. However, the truth is that perfection is an unattainable standard, and striving for it only sets us up for disappointment and burnout.

Embracing imperfection in parenthood means letting go of unrealistic expectations and accepting ourselves and our children exactly as we are. It's about recognizing that it's okay to make mistakes, to have bad days, and to not have all the answers. By embracing our flaws and vulnerabilities, we create space for authenticity and connection in our relationships with our children.

One of the first steps in embracing imperfection is letting go of the myth of the perfect parent. Instead of striving for unattainable perfection, we can focus on being good enough parents—parents who show up for their children with love, compassion, and authenticity, even when we don't have all the answers or everything figured out.

Practical tips for letting go of perfectionism in parenthood abound. These may include practicing self-compassion and self-care, setting realistic expectations for ourselves and our children, and learning to prioritize what truly matters. By cultivating mindfulness and presence in our parenting journey, we can learn to appreciate the beauty of imperfection and embrace the messy, chaotic moments with an open heart and mind.

Embracing imperfection in parenthood allows us to model resilience and self-acceptance for our children. By showing them that it's okay to make mistakes and that failure is an inevitable part of learning and growth, we empower them to embrace their own imperfections and navigate life's challenges.

The gift of imperfection in parenthood is a reminder that our worth as parents is not defined by our ability to be perfect, but by our capacity to love, accept, and show up for our children as imperfect, flawed human beings. By embracing imperfection and letting go of unrealistic expectations, we create space for joy, connection, and growth in our parenting journey, ultimately enriching our lives and the lives of our children in profound and meaningful ways.

1.12 Embracing the Journey

Embracing the journey of parenthood is an acknowledgment of the profound and transformative experience it entails—the highs, the lows, and everything in between. It's a recognition that parenthood is not a destination but a continuous journey of growth, discovery, and connection—a journey that is as messy and chaotic as it is beautiful and fulfilling.

Throughout this journey, we encounter moments of profound joy and connection that serve as beacons of light in the midst of life's challenges. From the first time we hold our newborn in our arms to the countless bedtime stories, laughter-filled playtimes, and heart-to-heart conversations shared over the years, these moments remind us of the deep bond we share with our children and the immense love that fuels our journey as parents.

But parenthood is not without its struggles. We face countless obstacles and uncertainties along the way—sleepless nights, tantrums, doubts, and fears—that test our patience, resilience, and self-belief. Yet, it's often through these challenges that we discover our greatest strengths and capacities for love and compassion.

In celebrating the journey of parenthood, we reflect on the lessons we have learned and the growth we have experienced along the way. We learn to let go of perfectionism and embrace the beauty of imperfection, to prioritize presence and connection over productivity, and to trust in our intuition and innate wisdom as parents.

To fellow parents embarking on this journey, we offer words of encouragement and support. You are not alone in your struggles, your triumphs, or your moments of doubt. Parenthood is a shared experience— a journey that unites us in our joys and challenges, our hopes and dreams for our children's futures.

As we navigate the twists and turns of parenthood, let us hold onto the belief that the love we share with our children is the greatest gift of all. It is a love that transcends time and space, a love that sustains us through the darkest of days and illuminates the path forward with hope and possibility.

So, let us embrace the journey of parenthood in all its complexity and beauty, cherishing each moment, savoring each connection, and celebrating the incredible privilege of guiding another human being through life's adventures. For in the end, it is the journey itself—the messy, imperfect, wonderful chaos of it all—that shapes us into the parents—and the people—we are meant to be.

Chapter 2: Embracing the Role of Caregiver and Guide

Embracing the role of caregiver and guide as a parent involves wholeheartedly committing to nurturing and supporting the physical, emotional, and intellectual growth of one's children. As a caregiver, parents provide love, care, and protection, attending to their children's basic needs and fostering a safe and nurturing environment. As guides, parents offer guidance, wisdom, and support, helping their children navigate life's challenges, learn important life skills, and develop into confident and responsible individuals. This dual role requires patience, empathy, and a deep sense of responsibility to help children flourish and thrive.

2.1 Understanding the Role of Caregiver

Understanding the role of a parent in caregiving involves recognizing the multifaceted nature of the parent-child relationship and the myriad ways in which parents provide love, support, and assistance to their children. At its core, caregiving encompasses not only meeting the basic physical needs of children but also attending to their emotional well-being, fostering their growth and development, and nurturing a strong bond built on trust and mutual respect.

Meeting the basic physical needs of children is one of the fundamental responsibilities of parenting. This includes providing food, shelter, clothing, and ensuring access to healthcare and other essential resources. However, caregiving goes beyond mere provision of necessities—it involves creating a safe and nurturing environment where children feel loved, valued, and supported.

Emotional support and comfort are equally essential aspects of caregiving. Parents play a crucial role in helping children navigate their emotions, offering reassurance, validation, and guidance during times of distress. By practicing empathy, compassion, and active listening, parents can create a supportive atmosphere where children feel understood and accepted, fostering their emotional resilience and well-being.

Caregiving also involves guiding and nurturing children's growth and development, helping them cultivate essential life skills and values. This may include teaching them how to communicate effectively, problem-solve, and navigate social relationships, as well as instilling values such as kindness, empathy, and resilience.

However, the role of a parent caregiver is not without its challenges. Balancing the demands of caregiving with other responsibilities, navigating conflicting needs and priorities, and coping with feelings of exhaustion or burnout are common struggles that caregivers may encounter along the way. It's essential for parents to practice self-care, seek support when needed, and recognize the importance of their own well-being in order to effectively care for their children.

Through personal anecdotes and reflective exercises, we can illuminate the profound impact that caregiving can have on both the caregiver and the recipient of care. From the joy of witnessing a child's growth and accomplishments to the profound sense of fulfillment that comes from nurturing a strong bond of love and trust, caregiving is a deeply meaningful and transformative experience that shapes both parent and child in profound ways.

2.2 Nurturing Growth and Development

Nurturing child growth and development is a central aspect of caregiving, as caregivers serve as guides and mentors in shaping the future of the individuals under their care. Effective guidance involves a thoughtful and intentional approach to fostering independence, autonomy, and resilience in children, while providing the support and encouragement they need to thrive.

At the heart of effective guidance is the principle of fostering independence and autonomy in children. Caregivers play a crucial role in helping children develop the skills and confidence they need to navigate the world with increasing independence. This may involve encouraging them to take on age-appropriate responsibilities, make decisions, and solve problems on their own, while providing guidance and support as needed.

Setting clear expectations and boundaries is another essential aspect of effective guidance. By establishing clear guidelines for behavior and communication, caregivers create a structured and predictable environment that promotes a sense of safety and security for children. Clear expectations help children understand what is expected of them and provide a framework for learning and growth.

In addition to setting expectations, caregivers also play a key role in providing encouragement, praise, and constructive feedback. Positive reinforcement and praise for effort and progress help build children's self-esteem and motivation, while constructive feedback helps them learn from mistakes and grow. By offering a balance of support and challenge, caregivers empower children to take healthy risks, learn from their experiences, and develop resilience in the face of adversity.

Real-life examples and case studies can help illustrate the transformative impact of effective guidance on children's growth and development. From the teenager who gains confidence and self-reliance through participating in extracurricular activities to the preschooler who learns to regulate their emotions and communicate effectively through positive reinforcement and modeling, these examples highlight the power of effective guidance in empowering children to reach their full potential.

Nurturing child growth and development requires caregivers to approach their role with intentionality, empathy, and patience. By providing a supportive and nurturing environment, setting clear expectations and boundaries, and offering encouragement and constructive feedback, caregivers can empower children to become resilient, confident, and compassionate individuals who are equipped to navigate life's challenges.

2.3 Cultivating Trust and Connection

Cultivating trust and connection between parent and child is essential for fostering a strong and healthy relationship built on mutual respect and understanding. At the core of this relationship lies the caregiver-guide bond—a dynamic connection characterized by trust, empathy, and authenticity. By prioritizing trust and connection, parents can create a nurturing environment where children feel safe, valued, and supported in their growth and development.

Consistency, reliability, and honesty are fundamental pillars of building trust between parent and child. Consistency involves following through on promises and expectations, providing a sense of stability and predictability that children can rely on. Reliability means being there for our children when they need us, whether it's for emotional support, guidance, or practical assistance. Honesty entails being open and transparent in our communication, even when it's difficult, and modeling integrity and authenticity in our actions.

Empathy and understanding also play a crucial role in fostering trust and connection between parent and child. By actively listening to our children's thoughts, feelings, and concerns, and validating their experiences without judgment, we demonstrate our empathy and understanding. This creates a safe and supportive space where children feel heard, understood, and accepted, strengthening the bond between parent and child.

Interactive exercises and role-playing scenarios can be valuable tools for exploring practical techniques for building trust and connection between parent and child. These exercises may involve practicing active listening skills, expressing gratitude and appreciation, and engaging in collaborative problem-solving. Through hands-on activities, parents can learn to better understand their children's perspectives and needs, strengthen communication skills, and deepen the bond of trust and connection.

Cultivating trust and connection between parent and child is an ongoing process that requires intentionality, empathy, and patience. By prioritizing consistency, reliability, honesty, empathy, and understanding, parents can create a nurturing and supportive environment where children feel valued, respected, and empowered to thrive. In doing so, they lay the foundation for a strong and resilient relationship built on trust, connection, and mutual love and respect.

2.4 Fostering Resilience and Adaptability

Fostering resilience and adaptability in children is crucial for equipping them with the skills and mindset needed to navigate life's challenges and uncertainties. As parents, we play a vital role in nurturing these qualities in our children, helping them develop the resilience and adaptability they need to thrive in an ever-changing world.

Resilience is the ability to bounce back from adversity, to persevere in the face of setbacks, and to emerge stronger and more resilient than before. By fostering resilience in our children, we empower them to cope with stress, overcome obstacles, and thrive in the face of adversity. This involves teaching them healthy coping mechanisms, such as problem-solving skills, positive self-talk, and seeking support from others. It also entails modeling resilience in our own lives, demonstrating perseverance and optimism in the face of challenges.

Adaptability is another essential quality for children to develop, as it enables them to respond effectively to changing circumstances and needs. In today's rapidly evolving world, adaptability is a valuable skill that allows children to navigate uncertainty and embrace new opportunities with confidence and flexibility. Parents can foster adaptability in their children by encouraging them to embrace change, take healthy risks, and learn from their experiences. This may involve exposing children to new experiences, encouraging them to try new things, and providing them with opportunities for growth and exploration.

Personal stories of resilience and adaptability can serve as powerful examples for children, illustrating how these qualities can empower individuals to overcome obstacles and thrive in the face of adversity. By sharing our own experiences of facing challenges and navigating change, we can inspire our children to develop resilience and adaptability in their own lives.

Fostering resilience and adaptability in children is about empowering them to navigate life's ups and downs with confidence and resilience. By teaching them healthy coping mechanisms, modeling resilience in our own lives, and providing them with opportunities for growth and exploration, parents can help their children develop the skills and mindset needed to thrive in an ever-changing world. In doing so, we empower our children to face life's challenges with courage, resilience, and optimism, knowing that they have the tools and support they need to succeed.

2.5 Balancing Self-Care and Caregiving

Balancing self-care with the responsibilities of caregiving and guiding is essential for parents to maintain their well-being and effectively support their children's growth and development. Self-care is not selfish; it's a fundamental aspect of being able to show up as the best version of ourselves for our children. By prioritizing self-care, parents can replenish their energy, reduce stress, and foster resilience, ultimately enhancing their ability to provide nurturing care and guidance to their children.

Setting boundaries is a critical aspect of balancing self-care with caregiving responsibilities. This involves recognizing and respecting our own limits and needs, and communicating them clearly to others. By setting boundaries around our time, energy, and personal space, parents can ensure that they have the resources they need to care for themselves while also meeting the needs of their children.

Managing stress is another essential component of self-care for parents. Parenthood can be challenging and demanding, and it's natural for parents to experience stress and overwhelm at times. By practicing stress management techniques such as deep breathing, mindfulness, or exercise, parents can reduce stress levels and increase their resilience in the face of challenges.

Seeking support from others is also crucial for balancing self-care with caregiving responsibilities. Parenthood is not meant to be a solitary journey, and parents can benefit from the support and assistance of friends, family members, or support groups. By reaching out for help when needed, parents can alleviate some of the burdens of caregiving and create space for self-care and personal fulfillment.

Self-care assessments and mindfulness exercises can be valuable tools for parents to explore practical techniques for promoting self-care and preventing burnout. These exercises may involve reflecting on their own needs and priorities, identifying areas where they can make self-care a priority, and developing a self-care plan that aligns with their values and goals.

Balancing self-care with the responsibilities of caregiving and guiding is about recognizing the importance of nurturing our own well-being in order to better support the well-being of our children. By prioritizing self-care, setting boundaries, managing stress, and seeking support from others, parents can create a sustainable and fulfilling parenting journey that benefits both themselves and their children.

2.6 Embracing the Transformative Power of Caregiving and Guiding

Embracing the transformative power of child caregiving and guiding is a profound acknowledgment of the immense impact that parents have on the lives of their children and themselves. It's recognizing that caregiving and guiding are not just tasks to be checked off a list, but journeys of growth, connection, and discovery that shape us in profound ways.

Throughout this journey, parents experience moments of joy, connection, and growth that remind us of the profound privilege and responsibility of nurturing another human being. From the first time we hold our newborn in our arms to the countless milestones along the way, these moments serve as poignant reminders of the deep bond we share with our children and the profound love that fuels our journey as parents.

However, caregiving and guiding are not without their challenges. From sleepless nights to tantrums and tears, parents encounter obstacles and uncertainties along the way that test our patience, resilience, and self-belief. Yet, it's often through these challenges that we discover our greatest strengths and capacities for love and compassion.

In reflecting on the transformative power of caregiving and guiding, we celebrate the resilience, empathy, and authenticity that emerge as we navigate the highs and lows of parenthood. We recognize the ways in which caregiving and guiding have shaped us into more compassionate, patient, and resilient individuals, capable of facing life's challenges.

Through personal reflections and words of encouragement, we inspire parents to embrace their roles with compassion, authenticity, and resilience. We remind them that their efforts have the power to shape lives and empower futures, not only for their children but also for themselves. By nurturing a strong bond of love and trust with their children, parents can create a foundation for growth, resilience, and well-being that will serve them both throughout their lives.

Embracing the transformative power of child caregiving and guiding is about recognizing the profound impact that parents have on the lives of their children and themselves. It's about celebrating the moments of joy, connection, and growth that accompany the caregiving and guiding process, while also acknowledging the challenges that help us learn and grow. By approaching parenthood with compassion, authenticity, and resilience, parents can create a nurturing and supportive environment where children can thrive and flourish, ultimately shaping the future for generations to come.

Chapter 3: Setting the Foundation for a Loving and Supportive Family Environment

Setting the foundation for a loving and supportive family environment is a journey filled with love, challenges, and transformative moments. It is important to celebrate the moments of joy, connection, and resilience that shapes our family journey, as well as the challenges that strengthen our bonds and test our resilience. Through reflection and gratitude, we can affirm our commitment to nurturing a loving and supportive family environment that empowers every family member to thrive and flourish.

3.1 The Power of Love and Connection

The power of love and connection in a family is unparalleled, serving as the foundation upon which strong, resilient bonds are formed and nurtured. Love permeates every aspect of family life, from the intimate moments shared between parents and children to the bonds of siblinghood and friendship that flourish within the family unit.

At its core, love is a transformative force that fosters connection, intimacy, and belonging within the family. It transcends words and actions, permeating the very essence of our relationships and shaping the dynamics of family life in profound ways. Unconditional parental love, in particular, is a powerful force that provides children with a sense of security, acceptance, and worthiness, laying the groundwork for healthy emotional development and lifelong resilience.

Beyond parental love, the bonds of siblinghood and friendship also play a significant role in fostering love and connection within the family. Siblings share a unique bond forged through shared experiences, memories, and mutual support, offering each other companionship, empathy, and understanding as they navigate the ups and downs of life together. Likewise, friendships within the family—whether between parents, siblings, or extended relatives—contribute to a sense of belonging and support, enriching the fabric of family life with laughter, camaraderie, and shared experiences.

Personal anecdotes and reflective exercises can serve as powerful tools for illuminating the profound impact that love has on shaping family relationships. By sharing stories of love, connection, and resilience within the family, we gain insight into the transformative power of love in nurturing strong, healthy bonds that withstand the test of time and adversity. Through these exercises, we can deepen our appreciation for the unique strengths and dynamics of our own family relationships, fostering a sense of gratitude and connection that strengthens our bonds even further.

The power of love and connection in a family is undeniable, serving as the bedrock upon which strong, resilient relationships are built. By embracing the transformative power of love, we create a nurturing and supportive environment where every family member feels valued, accepted, and cherished. Through the bonds of love and connection, families find solace, strength, and joy, enriching their lives and shaping their shared journey with warmth, compassion, and enduring affection.

3.2 Cultivating Open Communication

Cultivating open communication between parents and children is vital for fostering trust, resolving conflicts, and nurturing strong, meaningful connections within the family. When communication channels are open and honest, parents and children can better understand each other's perspectives, express their thoughts and feelings freely, and collaborate to address challenges and build stronger relationships.

Effective communication begins with active listening—a skill that involves paying full attention to what the other person is saying, without interrupting or jumping to conclusions. By practicing active listening, parents can demonstrate empathy and understanding, validating their children's experiences and feelings, and creating a safe space for open dialogue.

Expressing thoughts and feelings with honesty and empathy is another crucial aspect of open communication. Parents can model healthy communication by being transparent about their own thoughts and emotions, while also encouraging their children to express themselves openly and honestly. By creating an environment where all voices are valued and respected, parents can empower their children to communicate authentically and assertively.

Role-playing scenarios and communication exercises can be valuable tools for demonstrating the principles of open communication within the family. These exercises may involve practicing active listening skills, expressing thoughts and feelings through role-playing, and brainstorming solutions to hypothetical conflicts or challenges. By engaging in these activities together, parents and children can learn to communicate more effectively, navigate disagreements with respect and empathy, and strengthen their bonds as a family.

Cultivating open communication between parents and children is about creating a supportive and harmonious family environment where everyone feels heard, understood, and valued. By prioritizing active listening, honesty, and empathy, parents can foster a culture of open communication that strengthens family bonds, promotes trust and understanding, and lays the foundation for healthy relationships that endure through life's ups and downs.

3.3 Establishing Rituals and Traditions

Establishing rituals and traditions in a family is about more than just going through the motions—it's about creating meaningful experiences that bring family members together, foster a sense of belonging, and strengthen the bonds of love and connection. Whether it's a daily routine, a holiday celebration, or a special family ritual, these practices serve as the glue that binds families together, providing a sense of continuity, identity, and shared history.

One of the key benefits of establishing rituals and traditions within the family unit is the sense of continuity they provide. In a world that often feels fast-paced and ever-changing, family rituals offer a sense of stability and predictability that can be comforting and grounding for both children and adults alike. Whether it's a weekly family game night, a monthly movie marathon, or a yearly camping trip, these rituals create a sense of routine and familiarity that helps strengthen family bonds and create lasting memories.

Moreover, rituals and traditions also play a crucial role in shaping family identity and fostering a sense of belonging. By participating in shared rituals and traditions, family members create a sense of unity and solidarity that reinforces their connection to one another and to their family heritage. Whether it's cooking a favorite family recipe passed down through generations, or celebrating a cultural holiday or milestone, these rituals help families connect to their roots and instill a sense of pride in their shared identity.

Storytelling and memory-sharing exercises can be powerful tools for exploring the significance of rituals and traditions within the family. By sharing stories and reminiscing about past experiences, family members can deepen their understanding of the values, beliefs, and traditions that are important to their family culture. These exercises not only strengthen family bonds but also create opportunities for reflection, gratitude, and connection as family members come together to celebrate their shared history and experiences.

Establishing rituals and traditions in a family is essential for fostering connection, creating lasting memories, and nurturing a sense of belonging. By prioritizing these practices and incorporating them into family life, parents can create a supportive and harmonious environment where family members feel valued, understood, and connected to one another. Through storytelling, memory-sharing, and intentional participation in family rituals, families can strengthen their bonds and create a legacy of love and connection that endures for generations to come.

3.4 Nurturing Empathy and Understanding

Nurturing empathy and understanding within a family is essential for fostering strong, healthy relationships built on compassion, respect, and mutual support. Empathy—the ability to understand and share the feelings of others—is the foundation of compassion and understanding within the family unit, forming the basis for meaningful connections and fostering a supportive and caring family environment.

Teaching perspective-taking skills is a key strategy for nurturing empathy among family members. By encouraging children to consider the thoughts, feelings, and perspectives of others, parents can help them develop a greater understanding and appreciation for the experiences of their family members. This can be done through activities such as role-playing, storytelling, and asking open-ended questions that encourage children to put themselves in someone else's shoes.

Modeling empathy through acts of kindness and compassion is another effective way to nurture empathy within the family. When parents demonstrate empathy in their interactions with family members—whether it's comforting a sibling who is upset, listening attentively to a child's concerns, or offering support to a family member in need—they set a powerful example that teaches children the importance of empathy and compassion in relationships.

Empathy-building exercises and role-playing scenarios can also be valuable tools for fostering empathy within the family. These exercises may involve engaging in activities that promote perspective-taking, such as writing letters from the perspective of different family members or discussing how characters in books or movies might be feeling and why. Through these activities, family members can develop a deeper understanding of each other's experiences and feelings, leading to greater empathy and connection.

Nurturing empathy and understanding within a family is about creating a supportive and caring environment where every family member feels valued, heard, and understood. By teaching perspective-taking skills, modeling empathy through acts of kindness and compassion, and engaging in empathy-building exercises, parents can cultivate deeper connections and foster mutual respect within the family. In doing so, they lay the foundation for strong, healthy relationships built on empathy, understanding, and love.

3.5 Setting Boundaries with Love

Setting boundaries in a family with love is a delicate yet crucial aspect of maintaining healthy dynamics and fostering individual autonomy and self-expression. Boundaries serve as the invisible lines that define acceptable behaviors, interactions, and limits within the family unit. When set with love and respect, boundaries create a framework for mutual respect, understanding, and emotional safety, ultimately contributing to a harmonious and supportive family environment where each member feels valued, heard, and respected.

One of the fundamental aspects of setting boundaries with love is establishing clear expectations and guidelines for behavior within the family. This involves communicating openly and honestly with family members about what is and isn't acceptable, and why certain boundaries are important for maintaining harmony and well-being. By setting clear expectations, parents create a sense of predictability and consistency that helps children understand the rules and limits of their family environment.

Enforcing boundaries with empathy and understanding is another essential component of setting boundaries with love. While it's important to uphold boundaries and enforce consequences when necessary, it's equally important to do so with empathy and compassion. This involves acknowledging and validating the feelings and perspectives of family members, even when conflicts arise, and approaching boundary-setting from a place of love and respect rather than judgment or punishment.

Setting boundaries with love also means being flexible and willing to adapt as family dynamics and circumstances change. While it's important to establish firm boundaries to promote consistency and stability, it's also essential to recognize that boundaries may need to evolve over time to accommodate the changing needs and preferences of family members. By remaining open to feedback and communication, parents can ensure that boundaries are fair, reasonable, and aligned with the values and goals of the family as a whole.

Boundary-setting exercises can be valuable tools for exploring practical strategies for navigating boundary issues and promoting healthy boundaries within the family. These exercises may involve role-playing scenarios, discussing real-life examples of boundary-setting challenges, and brainstorming solutions together as a family. Through these activities, family members can develop a deeper understanding of the importance of boundaries and learn effective communication and problem-solving skills for addressing boundary issues in a constructive and respectful manner.

Setting boundaries in a family with love is about creating a supportive and nurturing environment where each member feels valued, respected, and heard. By establishing clear expectations, enforcing boundaries with empathy and understanding, and remaining open to feedback and communication, parents can promote mutual respect and emotional safety within the family. In doing so, they lay the foundation for healthy relationships, effective communication, and overall well-being for all family members.

3.6 Cultivating a Culture of Gratitude and Appreciation

Cultivating a culture of gratitude and appreciation within a family is not merely a feel-good practice; it is the cornerstone of building a positive, supportive, and harmonious environment where each member feels valued, acknowledged, and loved. Gratitude and appreciation have the power to transform family dynamics, fostering deeper connections, promoting resilience, and enhancing overall well-being.

Gratitude is the practice of recognizing and acknowledging the blessings, big and small, that enrich our lives. Within the family context, gratitude extends beyond mere words of thanks; it encompasses a mindset of appreciation for the unique contributions, efforts, and qualities of each family member. By cultivating a culture of gratitude, families can create a ripple effect of positivity and warmth that permeates every aspect of their interactions.

Expressing gratitude for small acts of kindness is one of the foundational practices for nurturing gratitude within the family. Whether it's a simple "thank you" for washing the dishes or a heartfelt note of appreciation for a supportive gesture, acknowledging and valuing the efforts of family members cultivates a sense of connection and validation. These expressions of gratitude serve as affirmations of love and appreciation, strengthening the bonds between family members and reinforcing positive behaviors.

Celebrating achievements and milestones is another powerful way to foster gratitude within the family. Whether it's a child's academic success, a parent's career milestone, or a family achievement such as completing a project together, celebrating accomplishments creates opportunities for joy, pride, and gratitude. By recognizing and commemorating these moments of growth and success, families can cultivate a culture of appreciation for each other's efforts and accomplishments, reinforcing a sense of unity and shared purpose.

Gratitude journaling is a practical technique for cultivating gratitude within the family. Encouraging family members to keep a gratitude journal, where they can write down three things they are grateful for each day, provides a tangible reminder of the abundance and blessings in their lives. By reflecting on the positive aspects of their day and expressing gratitude in writing, family members can cultivate a mindset of appreciation and abundance that extends beyond the journal pages into their daily interactions and relationships.

Gratitude-sharing exercises offer another avenue for nurturing gratitude within the family. These exercises may involve gathering as a family to share what they are grateful for, whether it's during mealtime conversations, bedtime rituals, or dedicated family meetings. By creating space for family members to express their gratitude openly and authentically, families can strengthen their connections, deepen their understanding of each other, and foster a sense of unity and belonging.

Practicing gratitude within the family is not only about acknowledging the positive aspects of life; it's also about embracing gratitude as a way of being—an attitude that shapes how we perceive and interact with the world around us. By cultivating a culture of gratitude and appreciation within the family, parents instill in their children a foundational value that fosters resilience, promotes empathy, and enhances overall well-being.

Cultivating a culture of gratitude and appreciation within the family is a transformative practice that enriches relationships, nurtures resilience, and fosters a sense of abundance and well-being. By expressing gratitude for small acts of kindness, celebrating achievements and milestones, journaling about gratitude, and sharing gratitude openly as a family, parents can create a supportive and harmonious environment where every member feels valued, acknowledged, and loved. Through these practices, families can cultivate deeper connections, strengthen bonds, and build a foundation of positivity and warmth that sustains them through life's ups and downs.

3.7 Promoting Emotional Resilience and Well-Being

Promoting emotional resilience and well-being within the family unit is crucial for equipping family members with the tools and skills needed to navigate life's challenges and setbacks with fortitude and resilience. Emotional resilience—the ability to bounce back from adversity, cope with stress, and adapt to change—is a fundamental aspect of mental and emotional health that influences how individuals respond to adversity and thrive in the face of difficulties.

Validating emotions is one of the foundational practices for promoting emotional resilience within the family. When family members feel heard, understood, and supported in expressing their emotions, they develop a sense of trust and safety that enables them to navigate challenges more effectively. Validating emotions involves acknowledging and accepting the full range of feelings—whether positive or negative—without judgment or criticism. By creating an environment where emotions are valued and respected, parents lay the groundwork for building emotional resilience and well-being within the family.

Teaching coping skills and problem-solving strategies is another essential aspect of promoting emotional resilience within the family. By equipping family members with practical tools and techniques for managing stress, regulating emotions, and solving problems, parents empower them to navigate life's challenges with confidence and resilience. Coping skills may include relaxation techniques such as deep breathing or mindfulness, strategies for challenging negative thoughts or beliefs, and activities that promote self-care and emotional regulation. By teaching these skills early on and modeling healthy coping behaviors, parents can foster a culture of resilience and well-being within the family.

Creating a supportive and resilient family environment involves fostering open communication and mutual support among family members. By encouraging family members to express their thoughts, feelings, and concerns openly and honestly, parents create opportunities for dialogue, connection, and validation. This open communication helps family members feel connected and supported, reducing feelings of isolation and promoting a sense of belonging and security. Moreover, by providing emotional support and encouragement during difficult times, family members can strengthen their bonds and build resilience together as a unit.

Resilience-building exercises offer practical techniques for promoting emotional well-being and resilience within the family. These exercises may involve role-playing scenarios, problem-solving activities, or guided imagery exercises that help family members practice coping skills and build resilience in a safe and supportive environment. By engaging in these exercises together, families can strengthen their bonds, develop new skills, and build a foundation of emotional resilience that sustains them through life's challenges.

Promoting emotional resilience and well-being within the family is a transformative practice that strengthens family bonds, fosters mutual support, and cultivates a culture of resilience and well-being. By validating emotions, teaching coping skills and problem-solving strategies, fostering open communication, and engaging in resilience-building exercises, parents can create a supportive and resilient family environment where every member feels empowered to navigate life's challenges. Through these practices, families can build stronger connections, enhance their emotional well-being, and thrive together as a resilient and cohesive unit.

3.8 Embracing Diversity and Inclusivity

Embracing diversity and inclusivity within the family, particularly due to intercultural marriage or international adoption, is not just about acknowledging differences—it's about celebrating them, actively challenging stereotypes and biases, and creating a supportive and inclusive environment where every family member feels valued, respected, and accepted for who they are. Diversity—the recognition and appreciation of the unique qualities, backgrounds, and perspectives that each family member brings to the table—is a cornerstone of healthy family dynamics, fostering understanding, empathy, and connection.

Celebrating cultural differences is one of the foundational practices for promoting diversity and inclusivity within the family. By recognizing and honoring the diverse cultural backgrounds, traditions, and customs of family members, parents create opportunities for learning, growth, and mutual respect. This may involve incorporating cultural traditions into family celebrations and rituals, learning about different cultural practices and beliefs, and exploring multicultural literature, music, and art together as a family. By embracing cultural diversity, families not only broaden their perspectives but also deepen their connections and foster a sense of belonging and acceptance among family members.

Challenging stereotypes and biases is another essential aspect of promoting diversity and inclusivity within the family. Stereotypes and biases—preconceived notions or beliefs about certain groups of people based on characteristics such as race, ethnicity, gender, or religion—can perpetuate harmful attitudes and behaviors that undermine inclusivity and respect. By engaging in open and honest conversations about stereotypes and biases, parents can help family members recognize and challenge these harmful beliefs, fostering empathy, understanding, and acceptance. This may involve discussing media representations, exploring personal experiences, and actively seeking out diverse perspectives and voices to counteract stereotypes and promote inclusivity within the family.

Creating a supportive and inclusive family environment involves fostering empathy, compassion, and respect among family members. By encouraging empathy, parents help family members develop a deeper appreciation for the experiences, perspectives, and struggles of others. This may involve engaging in perspective-taking exercises, practicing active listening, and modeling inclusive behaviors such as kindness, fairness, and tolerance. By fostering a culture of empathy and respect, parents create a safe and supportive space where every family member feels valued, understood, and accepted for who they are.

Embracing diversity and inclusivity within the family is a transformative practice that strengthens family bonds, fosters empathy and understanding, and promotes a sense of belonging and acceptance among family members. By celebrating cultural differences, challenging stereotypes and biases, fostering empathy and respect, parents can create a supportive and inclusive family environment where every member feels valued, respected, and accepted for who they are. Through these practices, families can build stronger connections, enhance their cultural competence, and create a legacy of inclusivity and respect that enriches their lives and the lives of future generations.

3.9 Fostering Collaboration and Teamwork

Fostering collaboration and teamwork within the family is not just about working together towards common goals—it's about building strong, supportive relationships, nurturing communication skills, and fostering a sense of unity and cooperation among family members. Collaboration—the act of working together towards shared objectives—promotes a culture of mutual respect, understanding, and support within the family unit, ultimately strengthening bonds and creating a harmonious family environment where everyone feels valued and empowered.

Assigning roles and responsibilities is one of the foundational practices for promoting collaboration within the family. By involving family members in decision-making processes and assigning tasks and responsibilities based on individual strengths and interests, parents empower them to take ownership of their contributions and actively participate in family life. This may involve creating chore charts, rotating household duties, or assigning specific roles and responsibilities for family projects and activities. By sharing the workload and working together towards common goals, family members develop a sense of accountability and teamwork that strengthens family bonds and promotes a culture of collaboration and cooperation.

Resolving conflicts and making decisions collectively is another essential aspect of fostering collaboration within the family. Conflicts are a natural part of family life, but how they are managed and resolved can significantly impact family dynamics. By promoting open communication, active listening, and respectful dialogue, parents create opportunities for family members to express their thoughts, feelings, and concerns constructively and work together to find mutually beneficial solutions. This may involve holding family meetings to discuss issues and concerns, establishing ground rules for respectful communication, and teaching conflict resolution skills such as compromise, negotiation, and problem-solving. By approaching conflicts and decisions as opportunities for learning and growth, families can strengthen their bonds, build trust, and foster a culture of collaboration and teamwork.

Teamwork-building exercises offer practical techniques for promoting collaboration and teamwork within the family. These exercises may involve engaging in team-building activities, such as scavenger hunts, cooperative games, or group projects, that require family members to work together towards a common objective. By participating in these activities, families can develop essential teamwork skills, such as communication, cooperation, and problem-solving, while also strengthening their bonds and creating lasting memories together. Through these exercises, family members learn to trust and rely on each other, cultivate a sense of unity and solidarity, and develop a shared sense of purpose and accomplishment that enhances family cohesion and resilience.

Fostering collaboration and teamwork within the family is a transformative practice that strengthens family bonds, promotes communication and problem-solving skills, and cultivates a culture of unity and cooperation. By assigning roles and responsibilities, resolving conflicts, making decisions collectively, and engaging in teamwork-building exercises, parents can create a supportive and harmonious family environment where every member feels valued, empowered, and connected. Through these practices, families can build stronger relationships, enhance their teamwork skills, and navigate challenges together, ultimately creating a foundation of unity and support that sustains them through life's ups and downs.

3.10 Creating a Safe and Supportive Space

Creating a safe and supportive space within the family is not just about physical safety—it's about nurturing emotional security, fostering open communication, and building trust and intimacy among family members. A safe and supportive family environment provides a foundation for growth, resilience, and well-being, where every member feels valued, respected, and accepted for who they are.

Establishing clear boundaries is one of the foundational practices for creating a safe and supportive space within the family. Boundaries define the limits of acceptable behavior, interactions, and expectations within the family unit, providing structure and predictability that promote a sense of safety and security. By communicating openly and honestly about family rules, expectations, and values, parents create a framework for respectful and healthy relationships among family members. This may involve discussing topics such as privacy, personal space, and respect for others' feelings and boundaries, and establishing consequences for violating family rules. By setting clear boundaries and enforcing them consistently, parents create a safe and supportive environment where every member feels respected and protected.

Addressing safety concerns is another essential aspect of creating a safe and supportive space within the family. Safety concerns can encompass a wide range of issues, including physical safety, emotional well-being, and protection from harm. By actively addressing potential safety risks and hazards, parents help ensure the physical and emotional well-being of their family members. This may involve implementing safety measures such as childproofing the home, teaching children about personal safety and stranger danger, and addressing issues such as bullying, peer pressure, and substance abuse. By prioritizing safety and well-being, parents create a nurturing environment where family members feel secure and protected.

Promoting open communication is key to creating a safe and supportive space within the family. Open communication involves listening attentively, expressing thoughts and feelings honestly and respectfully, and fostering a climate of trust and understanding among family members. By encouraging family members to communicate openly about their thoughts, feelings, and concerns, parents create opportunities for connection, validation, and support. This may involve holding regular family meetings to discuss important issues and decisions, establishing a culture of active listening and empathy, and providing opportunities for family members to share their experiences and perspectives without fear of judgment or criticism. By promoting open communication, parents create a safe and supportive space where every member feels heard, understood, and valued.

Safety planning and trust-building exercises offer practical techniques for creating a safe and supportive space within the family. Safety planning involves identifying potential risks and hazards, developing strategies for addressing them, and empowering family members to take proactive steps to protect themselves and each other. Trust-building exercises may involve engaging in activities that promote trust, such as team-building exercises, sharing personal stories and experiences, and engaging in acts of kindness and compassion. Through these exercises, families can strengthen their bonds, build trust and intimacy, and create a supportive environment where every member feels safe, supported, and valued.

Creating a safe and supportive space within the family is a transformative practice that strengthens family relationships, promotes emotional well-being, and fosters a sense of security and belonging among family members. By establishing clear boundaries, addressing safety concerns, promoting open communication, and engaging in safety planning and trust-building exercises, parents can create a nurturing environment where every member feels respected, protected, and supported. Through these practices, families can build stronger bonds, enhance their resilience, and create a foundation of trust and intimacy that sustains them through life's challenges.

Section 2: Building Strong Foundations

Chapter 4: The Importance of Early Childhood Development

Early childhood development is a critical period of growth and development that lays the foundation for lifelong well-being and success. From the importance of early relationships and experiences to the impact of supportive environments and interventions, the early years are a time of immense opportunity and potential. By investing in early childhood development and promoting holistic approaches to support the diverse needs of young children, we can ensure that all children have the opportunity to thrive and reach their full potential, and build a brighter future for generations to come.

4.1 Understanding Early Childhood Development

Early childhood development is a critical period that sets the stage for a child's future growth and success. It encompasses a multifaceted journey, marked by significant physical, cognitive, emotional, and social changes during the first few years of life. Exploring this intricate process provides insights into the profound impact of early experiences on neural connections, brain architecture, and overall development.

At the dawn of life, infancy heralds a remarkable journey of growth and discovery. From the moment of birth, infants embark on a trajectory of rapid physical development. They transition from fragile, dependent beings to resilient explorers, mastering fundamental skills such as grasping objects, rolling over, and eventually taking their first tentative steps. These early motor milestones not only signal physical maturation but also pave the way for further cognitive and social development.

Simultaneously, the infant brain undergoes extraordinary transformations, forging neural pathways at an astonishing pace. Every interaction, every touch, and every sound leaves an indelible imprint, shaping the intricate circuitry of the developing brain. Through the lens of neuroscience, we unravel the mysteries of synaptic pruning and neuroplasticity, understanding how early experiences sculpt the foundation of cognitive functioning and emotional regulation.

As infancy gives way to the toddler years, the child's burgeoning autonomy is accompanied by a burgeoning cognitive prowess. Curiosity becomes their constant companion, driving them to explore the world with insatiable wonder. Language blossoms, transforming babbling into coherent speech as toddlers navigate the complexities of communication. Meanwhile, their burgeoning imaginations ignite, fueling creative play and problem-solving skills.

Yet, alongside these cognitive leaps, toddlers grapple with the turbulent seas of emotion. Temper tantrums and tears punctuate their journey as they learn to navigate the intricate landscape of feelings. Through gentle guidance and empathetic support, caregivers play a pivotal role in helping toddlers regulate their emotions and build resilience in the face of adversity.

As the preschool years dawn, children embark on a new chapter of social exploration and self-discovery. Peer interactions become a central focus as they learn to navigate the complexities of friendship and cooperation. Preschoolers delight in imaginative play, transforming everyday objects into fantastical realms where dragons roam and adventures await.

Within this vibrant tapestry of development, case studies offer poignant insights into the interplay between biology and environment. From the resilient spirit of a child overcoming adversity to the transformative power of early interventions, these stories underscore the profound impact of nurturing relationships and enriching environments on developmental outcomes.

Through the lens of developmental milestones, we witness the intricate dance of nature and nurture shaping the trajectory of early childhood development. From the first tentative steps of infancy to the imaginative leaps of preschool, each milestone represents a triumph of growth and resilience. By understanding and supporting these critical junctures, we lay the foundation for future learning, behavior, and health.

Understanding early childhood development is paramount in unlocking the full potential of every child. By recognizing the interconnectedness of physical, cognitive, emotional, and social domains, we empower caregivers, educators, and policymakers to create nurturing environments that foster optimal development. As we delve into the depths of early childhood, we illuminate a path towards a brighter, more equitable future for generations to come.

4.2 The Role of Early Relationships and Attachment

In the intricate tapestry of early childhood development, the bond between parent and child stands as a cornerstone, shaping the very foundation of a child's growth and well-being. At the heart of this bond lies the concept of attachment, a dynamic and enduring emotional connection that forms the bedrock of healthy development.

Attachment, coined by psychologist John Bowlby, refers to the deep emotional bond that develops between infants and their primary caregivers, typically their parents. This bond serves as a secure base from which the child explores the world, seeks comfort in times of distress, and forms relationships with others. Secure attachments are characterized by caregivers who are responsive, consistent, and sensitive to their child's needs, fostering a sense of trust and emotional security.

Research findings underscore the pivotal role of secure attachments in promoting emotional well-being and healthy development. Children who form secure attachments with their caregivers demonstrate greater resilience in the face of adversity, exhibiting lower levels of anxiety and depression later in life. These early relationships provide a buffer against stress and trauma, offering a safe harbor in times of turmoil.

Real-life examples illuminate the transformative power of secure attachments in shaping a child's sense of self and relationships with others. From the tender embrace of a mother soothing her crying infant to the playful interactions between a father and his toddler, everyday moments become building blocks for emotional security and trust. These early experiences lay the groundwork for healthy social development, fostering empathy, compassion, and cooperation in relationships with peers and adults alike.

Conversely, insecure attachments, characterized by inconsistent caregiving or neglect, can have profound and lasting effects on a child's development. Children who experience insecure attachments may struggle with emotional regulation, exhibiting behaviors such as aggression or withdrawal in response to stress. Without a secure base to turn to, they may have difficulty forming trusting relationships and may experience challenges in navigating social interactions.

The impact of early relationships and attachment extends far beyond childhood, influencing the trajectory of development into adolescence and adulthood. Adolescents who have formed secure attachments with their caregivers are more likely to exhibit positive self-esteem, establish healthy relationships, and achieve academic success. Conversely, those who have experienced insecure attachments may face heightened risks of mental health issues, substance abuse, and difficulties in forming intimate relationships.

Understanding the critical role of early relationships and attachment underscores the importance of supporting caregivers in nurturing secure bonds with their children. Parenting interventions that promote sensitive and responsive caregiving can enhance attachment security and promote positive developmental outcomes. By providing caregivers with the knowledge and support they need to meet their child's emotional needs, we can foster environments that cultivate resilience, empathy, and emotional well-being.

The bond between parent and child is a powerful force that shapes the course of a child's development and well-being. Through the lens of attachment theory, we gain insights into the profound impact of early relationships on a child's sense of self, social development, and emotional regulation. By nurturing secure attachments and supporting caregivers, we lay the foundation for a future marked by resilience, empathy, and flourishing relationships.

4.3 Stimulating Environments and Learning Opportunities

The early years of childhood are akin to a canvas waiting to be painted upon, a time of boundless potential and rapid growth. Central to this developmental journey is the environment in which a child is nurtured and the opportunities for learning and exploration it provides.

A stimulating environment encompasses a rich tapestry of experiences that engage a child's senses, curiosity, and imagination. From the gentle rustle of leaves in a backyard garden to the vibrant colors of a picture book, every moment presents an opportunity for learning and discovery. Parents play a fundamental role in curating such environments, serving as architects of their child's early experiences.

At the heart of this environment lies the transformative power of play. Play is not merely a frivolous pastime but a cornerstone of early childhood development, providing a fertile ground for creativity, problem-solving skills, and social competence to flourish. Whether building towering block structures or embarking on imaginative adventures, children learn valuable lessons about collaboration, communication, and resilience through play.

Research underscores the myriad benefits of play in promoting cognitive, emotional, and social development. Children who engage in unstructured play exhibit greater creativity, cognitive flexibility, and emotional regulation skills. Moreover, play serves as a natural vehicle for learning, allowing children to explore mathematical concepts, scientific principles, and language skills in a meaningful context.

Beyond the home environment, early intervention programs and high-quality early childhood education play a pivotal role in providing enriching learning opportunities for children from diverse backgrounds. These programs serve as catalysts for closing achievement gaps and promoting school readiness, equipping children with the skills and competencies needed to thrive in formal educational settings.

Case studies and program evaluations offer compelling evidence of the transformative impact of enriching environments on early childhood outcomes. From the success stories of children who have benefited from early intervention programs to the positive effects of high-quality preschool education on academic achievement, these examples underscore the importance of investing in early childhood development.

In one such case study, a longitudinal evaluation of a home-visiting program for at-risk families revealed significant improvements in children's cognitive development, language skills, and social-emotional competence. By providing parents with guidance and support in fostering nurturing environments, the program empowered families to create lasting positive changes in their children's lives.

In another example, a comprehensive review of high-quality preschool programs highlighted their role in promoting school readiness and reducing disparities in educational achievement. Children who attended these programs demonstrated higher levels of early literacy and numeracy skills, as well as greater social competence and emotional resilience compared to their peers who did not have access to such opportunities.

Stimulating environments and learning opportunities are essential ingredients in nurturing healthy early childhood development. Parents, as primary caregivers and educators, play a central role in creating enriching experiences that foster curiosity, creativity, and resilience in their children. By embracing the transformative power of play and investing in high-quality early childhood education, we can pave the way for a future where every child has the opportunity to thrive and reach their full potential.

4.4 Promoting Physical Health and Well-Being

Physical health forms the cornerstone of early childhood development, laying the groundwork for lifelong well-being and flourishing. Within the nurturing embrace of a family, parents serve as stewards of their child's health, guiding them on a path towards optimal growth and vitality.

Nutrition stands as a fundamental pillar of physical health, providing the building blocks for growth, development, and overall vitality. From the first moments of infancy, breast milk or formula offers essential nutrients and antibodies crucial for immune function and brain development. As children transition to solid foods, parents play a vital role in shaping their dietary habits, introducing a diverse array of fruits, vegetables, whole grains, and lean proteins to nourish their growing bodies.

Research underscores the profound impact of early nutrition on long-term health outcomes, with poor dietary habits in childhood increasing the risk of obesity, chronic disease, and mental health disorders in later life. By prioritizing nutrient-dense foods and modeling healthy eating behaviors, parents can instill lifelong habits that promote physical health and well-being.

In addition to nutrition, adequate sleep is essential for supporting optimal growth, cognitive function, and emotional regulation in early childhood. Establishing consistent bedtime routines and creating a conducive sleep environment are vital strategies for promoting healthy sleep habits. Research has shown that insufficient sleep in childhood is associated with a myriad of adverse health outcomes, including impaired cognitive function, behavioral problems, and increased risk of obesity.

Parents play a central role in facilitating healthy sleep habits by setting consistent bedtimes, creating a calming bedtime routine, and providing a comfortable sleep environment free from distractions. By prioritizing adequate sleep, parents not only support their child's physical health but also lay the foundation for improved academic performance and emotional well-being.

Physical activity is another critical component of promoting physical health and well-being in early childhood. Regular exercise not only supports healthy growth and development but also enhances cognitive function, mood regulation, and social skills. Parents can encourage physical activity by providing opportunities for active play, outdoor exploration, and structured exercise programs tailored to their child's interests and abilities.

Public health initiatives play a vital role in promoting physical health and well-being in early childhood, providing resources and support to families in need. Programs such as WIC (Women, Infants, and Children) and SNAP-Ed (Supplemental Nutrition Assistance Program Education) offer nutrition education, counseling, and food assistance to low-income families, ensuring that all children have access to healthy food options.

Furthermore, early intervention programs target at-risk populations, providing support and resources to families facing challenges related to nutrition, sleep, and physical activity. These programs offer guidance on healthy lifestyle behaviors, promote access to nutritious foods, and provide opportunities for physical activity, ultimately reducing disparities in health outcomes and promoting health equity.

Promoting physical health and well-being in early childhood is a vital investment in lifelong wellness. Within the nurturing embrace of a family, parents play a central role in fostering healthy habits and creating environments that support optimal growth and development. By prioritizing nutrition, sleep, and physical activity, parents can empower their children to thrive and reach their full potential, laying the foundation for a lifetime of health and well-being.

4.5 Fostering Language and Literacy Development

Language and literacy skills form the bedrock of academic success and social interaction, serving as the gateway to knowledge, communication, and self-expression. Within the nurturing embrace of a family, parents play a central role in cultivating these essential skills, laying the foundation for a lifetime of learning and achievement.

Early language exposure is a cornerstone of language development, with infants and young children eagerly soaking up the sounds and rhythms of speech from their caregivers. From the soothing lullabies sung to newborns to the animated conversations shared at the dinner table, every interaction offers an opportunity for language learning. Parents serve as primary language models, providing a rich tapestry of vocabulary, syntax, and grammar that lays the groundwork for linguistic proficiency.

Research underscores the profound impact of early language exposure on language acquisition and comprehension, with children who experience a language-rich environment demonstrating greater vocabulary development, syntactic complexity, and reading comprehension skills. By engaging in responsive and interactive communication with their children, parents can nurture linguistic competence and foster a lifelong love of language and learning.

Conversation serves as a vehicle for language development, offering opportunities for children to practice communication skills, expand their vocabulary, and express their thoughts and ideas. By engaging in back-and-forth exchanges with their children, parents stimulate language development and promote cognitive growth. These dialogic interactions not only enhance language skills but also foster critical thinking, problem-solving, and social competence.

Storytelling holds a special place in the hearts of families, weaving tales of adventure, imagination, and wonder that captivate young minds and ignite a passion for reading. Shared reading experiences expose children to rich and varied language patterns, narrative structures, and literary conventions, laying the groundwork for literacy acquisition and comprehension. By incorporating storytelling into daily routines, parents instill a love of literature and provide children with the tools they need to become confident and proficient readers.

Early literacy interventions and language-rich environments play a vital role in promoting school readiness and academic achievement, providing targeted support to children who may be at risk for language and literacy difficulties. Programs such as "Reach Out and Read" and "Head Start" offer literacy-focused interventions and resources to families, equipping parents with the knowledge and skills they need to support their child's language and literacy development.

Through research findings and literacy programs, we gain insights into the transformative impact of early language and literacy experiences on cognitive development and educational outcomes. Longitudinal studies have shown that children who receive early intervention in language and literacy skills demonstrate improved academic performance, higher rates of literacy attainment, and greater success in school and beyond.

Fostering language and literacy development in the early years is a vital investment in a child's future success and well-being. Within the nurturing embrace of a family, parents serve as architects of their child's linguistic journey, providing the building blocks for academic achievement, social interaction, and lifelong learning. By prioritizing early language exposure, conversation, storytelling, and literacy-rich environments, parents empower their children to unlock the doors to knowledge, imagination, and endless possibilities.

4.6 Supporting Social and Emotional Development

Social and emotional skills are the bedrock upon which healthy relationships, self-esteem, and mental well-being are built. Within the nurturing embrace of a family, parents serve as guides and role models, shaping their child's ability to navigate the complexities of the social world with empathy, resilience, and self-assurance.

Emotional regulation lays the foundation for healthy social and emotional development, enabling children to identify, understand, and manage their emotions effectively. From the tumultuous tempest of toddler tantrums to the stormy seas of adolescent angst, parents play a pivotal role in helping their children navigate the full spectrum of emotions. By providing a safe and supportive environment for expressing emotions and teaching coping strategies such as deep breathing, mindfulness, and positive self-talk, parents empower their children to regulate their emotions and build emotional resilience.

Empathy serves as a cornerstone of healthy relationships, fostering compassion, understanding, and connection with others. Parents play a vital role in nurturing empathy by modeling kindness, empathy, and perspective-taking in their interactions with others. Through acts of kindness, volunteering, and discussions about emotions and perspectives, parents cultivate a sense of empathy and altruism in their children, laying the groundwork for meaningful relationships and social responsibility.

Social competence encompasses a range of skills and abilities that enable children to navigate social interactions, form friendships, and resolve conflicts effectively. From the playground to the classroom, children rely on social competence to navigate the complexities of peer relationships and group dynamics. Parents can support the development of social competence by providing opportunities for cooperative play, modeling positive social behaviors, and teaching conflict resolution skills such as active listening, compromise, and negotiation.

Social-emotional learning programs offer structured interventions and curricula designed to promote social and emotional development in children. These programs provide children with the skills and strategies they need to navigate social situations, manage their emotions, and build healthy relationships. By integrating social-emotional learning into school curricula and community programs, educators and policymakers can empower children with the tools they need to thrive academically, socially, and emotionally.

Early intervention strategies target at-risk populations and provide support and resources to children facing social and emotional difficulties. Programs such as play therapy, mindfulness-based interventions, and social skills training offer targeted support to children struggling with emotional regulation, social anxiety, and interpersonal relationships. By addressing social and emotional challenges early on, these interventions promote resilience, mental health, and well-being in children.

Through case studies and social-emotional curricula, we gain insights into the transformative impact of early social and emotional experiences on lifelong well-being. From the success stories of children who have thrived in nurturing and supportive environments to the positive outcomes of social-emotional learning programs in schools, these examples underscore the importance of supporting social and emotional development in the early years.

Supporting social and emotional development in the early years is a vital investment in a child's future success and well-being. Within the nurturing embrace of a family, parents play a central role in cultivating emotional resilience, empathy, and social competence in their children. By prioritizing emotional regulation, empathy, and social competence, parents empower their children to navigate the complexities of the social world with confidence, compassion, and resilience, laying the foundation for a lifetime of positive relationships, self-esteem, and well-being.

4.7 Addressing Disparities and Inequities

In the tapestry of early childhood development, every child deserves the opportunity to flourish, yet disparities in access to resources and opportunities persist, casting a shadow over the promise of a bright future.

Socioeconomic status serves as a powerful determinant of early childhood outcomes, shaping access to resources such as quality healthcare, nutritious food, safe housing, and educational opportunities. Children born into poverty face a myriad of challenges that hinder their development, from limited access to prenatal care and early childhood education to exposure to environmental toxins and chronic stress. These socioeconomic disparities contribute to profound gaps in health, cognitive development, and academic achievement, perpetuating cycles of intergenerational poverty and inequality.

Similarly, race and ethnicity intersect with socioeconomic status to compound disparities in early childhood development. Children of color disproportionately experience poverty and systemic discrimination, facing barriers to accessing high-quality healthcare, education, and social services. Structural racism permeates every facet of society, from healthcare systems that perpetuate disparities in maternal and infant mortality rates to educational institutions that perpetuate the school-to-prison pipeline for children of color. These inequities exact a heavy toll on the health, well-being, and life chances of children of color, perpetuating cycles of disadvantage and marginalization.

Systemic inequities manifest in multiple domains of early childhood development, exacerbating disparities in health, education, and social well-being. Children from marginalized communities are more likely to experience food insecurity, inadequate healthcare, substandard housing, and exposure to violence and trauma. These adverse experiences have profound and lasting effects on their physical health, cognitive development, and social-emotional well-being, perpetuating cycles of poverty and inequality across generations.

Addressing disparities and promoting equity in early childhood development requires a multifaceted approach that addresses the root causes of inequity and empowers communities to thrive. Targeted interventions such as home visiting programs, early childhood education initiatives, and family support services provide critical resources and support to families facing socioeconomic challenges. These programs offer parenting education, access to healthcare and social services, and early intervention for children at risk of developmental delays, laying the foundation for positive outcomes in the early years and beyond.

Policy reforms are essential for dismantling systemic barriers to equity in early childhood development. Investments in affordable housing, healthcare, childcare, and education can level the playing field for children from marginalized communities, ensuring that all children have access to the resources and opportunities they need to thrive. Furthermore, policies that address structural racism and promote diversity, equity, and inclusion in all aspects of society are essential for creating a more just and equitable future for all children.

Community partnerships play a vital role in advancing equity in early childhood development, fostering collaboration among stakeholders to address the unique needs and challenges facing diverse communities. By engaging parents, caregivers, educators, healthcare providers, policymakers, and community leaders in collective action, we can create a supportive ecosystem that nurtures the health, well-being, and potential of every child.

Addressing disparities and inequities in early childhood development is a moral and strategic imperative for building a more just and equitable society. By confronting the systemic barriers that perpetuate inequality and investing in strategies that promote equity and opportunity for all children, we can create a future where every child has the opportunity to thrive in the early years and beyond. Through research, advocacy, and collective action, we can build a brighter and more equitable future for generations to come.

4.8 Engaging Families and Communities

In the intricate web of early childhood development, families and communities serve as the bedrock upon which children's growth, learning, and well-being are nurtured. Recognizing the pivotal role they play, it's essential to explore the importance of engaging families and communities in promoting positive outcomes for young children.

Families are the first and most influential teachers in a child's life, shaping their early experiences and laying the foundation for future success. Family support programs offer a lifeline to parents, providing resources, guidance, and emotional support to navigate the challenges of parenthood. From prenatal education and breastfeeding support to parenting classes and home visiting programs, these initiatives empower parents with the knowledge and skills they need to nurture their child's development and foster positive parent-child relationships.

Parent education initiatives offer a pathway to empowerment, equipping parents with the tools and strategies they need to support their child's growth and development. Through workshops, seminars, and one-on-one coaching sessions, parents learn about child development, positive discipline techniques, and effective communication skills. By strengthening parenting capacity, these initiatives promote positive parent-child interactions and create a supportive environment that enhances children's well-being and resilience.

Community partnerships amplify the impact of family support programs and parent education initiatives, fostering collaboration among stakeholders to address the unique needs and challenges facing families. By forging alliances with healthcare providers, educators, social service agencies, and community organizations, families gain access to a comprehensive network of support services that address their physical, emotional, and social needs. These partnerships create a seamless continuum of care that ensures families receive the support they need to thrive.

Community empowerment is central to promoting positive outcomes for young children and families. Empowering communities to identify their strengths, assets, and resources fosters a sense of ownership and agency. Community-based initiatives leverage the collective wisdom and resources of local residents to address systemic barriers and create opportunities for positive change. By mobilizing grassroots efforts and building social capital, communities can create environments that support early childhood development and well-being.

Case studies and community-based initiatives offer compelling evidence of the transformative impact of family and community engagement on early childhood outcomes. From the success stories of families who have benefited from support programs to the collaborative efforts of communities working together to create nurturing environments for children, these examples underscore the importance of investing in family and community engagement as a catalyst for positive change.

Families and communities play a critical role in supporting early childhood development, serving as essential partners in creating environments that nurture the growth, learning, and well-being of young children. By investing in family support programs, parent education initiatives, community partnerships, and community empowerment, we can create a future where every child has the opportunity to thrive and reach their full potential. Through collaboration, compassion, and collective action, we can build strong foundations for a brighter tomorrow, where all children have the chance to flourish.

4.9 Investing in Early Childhood Development

In the journey of parenthood, families serve as the primary architects of their children's futures, shaping their growth, learning, and well-being from the earliest moments of life. Recognizing the profound impact of early childhood development, families play a pivotal role in investing in their children's future success.

Early childhood education stands as a cornerstone of lifelong learning and achievement, offering children a strong foundation upon which to build their academic and professional pursuits. By investing in high-quality early childhood education programs, families provide their children with the cognitive, social, and emotional skills they need to succeed in school and beyond. Research has shown that children who participate in early childhood education programs are more likely to graduate from high school, pursue higher education, and secure stable employment, leading to increased productivity and higher earning potential over the course of their lives.

Early childhood education has been linked to a range of positive outcomes that benefit individuals, families, and society as a whole. By fostering cognitive development, language skills, and social competence, early childhood education reduces the likelihood of involvement in crime and delinquency, leading to safer communities and reduced criminal justice costs. Additionally, early childhood education promotes better health outcomes, as children who receive high-quality early education are more likely to adopt healthy behaviors and access preventive healthcare services, reducing healthcare costs and improving overall well-being.

In addition to the economic benefits of early childhood education, early intervention programs offer a cost-effective means of addressing developmental delays and supporting children with special needs. By identifying and addressing developmental challenges early on, families can access targeted support services that enhance their child's development and improve long-term outcomes. Early intervention programs have been shown to yield significant returns on investment, as they reduce the need for costly special education services and support children in reaching their full potential.

Furthermore, investing in the early years yields long-term savings that extend beyond individual families to benefit society as a whole. By promoting school readiness, preventing chronic health conditions, investments in early childhood development generate substantial returns for taxpayers and policymakers. Economic analyses have demonstrated that every dollar invested in early childhood education and intervention programs yields significant returns in terms of increased economic productivity, reduced healthcare costs.

Policy evaluations provide further evidence of the importance of prioritizing early childhood development as a smart investment in the future. By implementing policies that support access to high-quality early education and intervention services, policymakers can create a more equitable and prosperous society for all. Investing in early childhood development not only benefits individual families but also strengthens communities, boosts economic growth, and builds a brighter future for generations to come.

Investing in early childhood development is a wise investment, offering significant returns for individuals, families, and society as a whole. By prioritizing high-quality early education, early intervention programs, and supportive family environments, families can lay the groundwork for their children's future success and well-being. Through economic analyses, policy evaluations, and a commitment to providing every child with the opportunity to thrive, families can build a strong foundation for a brighter tomorrow, one child at a time.

4.10 Promoting Holistic Approaches to Early Childhood Development

In the intricate tapestry of early childhood development, families stand as the primary architects of their children's growth, learning, and well-being. Recognizing the multifaceted nature of this journey, families play a pivotal role in promoting holistic approaches to early childhood development.

Holistic approaches to early childhood development recognize that children are complex beings with interconnected needs across multiple domains of development – physical, cognitive, social, emotional, and linguistic. Families serve as the cornerstone of holistic care, providing a nurturing environment that supports children's growth and well-being across these dimensions. By integrating health, education, and social services, families can address the diverse needs of their children in a comprehensive and coordinated manner, fostering optimal development and lifelong success.

Integrating health services into early childhood development ensures that children have access to preventive care, screenings, and interventions that promote physical and mental well-being. From well-child visits and immunizations to developmental screenings and mental health services, families play a crucial role in prioritizing their children's health needs and connecting them with appropriate resources and support. By fostering healthy habits, addressing medical concerns promptly, and promoting positive health behaviors, families lay the foundation for a lifetime of wellness.

Education is another essential component of holistic early childhood development, providing children with the knowledge, skills, and experiences they need to succeed in school and beyond. Families serve as partners in their children's education, creating a supportive learning environment at home and advocating for high-quality educational opportunities in their communities. By engaging in activities that promote literacy, numeracy, critical thinking, and creativity, families empower their children to become lifelong learners and confident problem-solvers.

Social services play a vital role in addressing the social, emotional, and economic needs of children and families, ensuring that they have access to the resources and support they need to thrive. From parenting classes and support groups to childcare assistance and housing subsidies, families can access a range of services that promote stability, resilience, and well-being. By connecting families with community resources, advocating for their rights, and addressing systemic barriers, families can create a nurturing environment that supports children's holistic development.

Interdisciplinary collaborations are essential for promoting holistic approaches to early childhood development, fostering collaboration among healthcare providers, educators, social workers, and community organizations. By working together to identify and address the unique needs of children and families, interdisciplinary teams can provide comprehensive support that addresses the complex interplay of factors influencing development. Through shared goals, coordinated services, and effective communication, interdisciplinary collaborations maximize the impact of interventions and promote positive outcomes for children and families.

Systems-level reforms are necessary for creating environments that support holistic approaches to early childhood development, ensuring that all children have access to the resources and opportunities they need to thrive. By advocating for policies that prioritize early childhood education, healthcare, and social services, families can create a more equitable and inclusive society where every child has the opportunity to reach their full potential. Through legislative advocacy, community organizing, and grassroots activism, families can drive systemic change that promotes holistic approaches to early childhood development.

Promoting holistic approaches to early childhood development is essential for nurturing the whole child and ensuring that every child has the opportunity to reach their full potential. By integrating health, education, and social services, families can address the diverse needs of children and families in a comprehensive and coordinated manner. Through interdisciplinary collaborations, systems-level reforms, and a commitment to holistic care, families can create environments that support children's growth, learning, and well-being, laying the foundation for a brighter future for generations to come.

Chapter 5: Nurturing Emotional Intelligence and Resilience

Emotional intelligence and resilience are essential qualities that enable individuals to navigate life's challenges. By nurturing emotional intelligence and resilience, individuals can cultivate greater self-awareness, empathy, and strength in the face of adversity. Through self-reflection, practice, and support, individuals can develop the skills and mindset needed to thrive in an ever-changing world.

5.1 Understanding Emotional Intelligence

Emotional intelligence (EI) stands as a cornerstone of personal and interpersonal success, empowering individuals to navigate the complexities of human relationships. In the journey of childhood development, understanding and cultivating EI are essential for laying the foundation for lifelong well-being and success. As parents, we illuminate the transformative power of emotional intelligence in shaping children's personal and professional trajectories.

At its core, emotional intelligence encompasses the ability to recognize, understand, and manage emotions effectively. Self-awareness forms the bedrock of EI, enabling children to identify and label their own emotions and understand how they influence thoughts, behaviors, and relationships. By fostering self-awareness, parents empower children to develop a deeper understanding of themselves and their emotional experiences, laying the groundwork for self-reflection, personal growth, and self-acceptance.

Self-regulation is another critical component of emotional intelligence, enabling children to manage their emotions, impulses, and reactions in a constructive manner. Through strategies such as deep breathing, mindfulness, and positive self-talk, children learn to regulate their emotions and behaviors, fostering resilience and coping skills in the face of adversity. By cultivating self-regulation, parents equip children with the tools they need to navigate challenges, setbacks, and conflicts effectively, promoting emotional well-being and mental health.

Empathy is the ability to understand and share the feelings of others, fostering compassion, connection, and cooperation in relationships. Empathetic children demonstrate a genuine concern for the well-being of others, offering support, comfort, and understanding in times of need. By teaching children to perspective-take, listen actively, and recognize the emotions of others, parents nurture empathy and promote positive social interactions, building strong foundations for healthy relationships and social competence.

Social skills encompass a range of abilities that enable children to communicate, collaborate, and resolve conflicts effectively in social settings. From active listening and assertive communication to cooperation and negotiation, social skills are essential for navigating the complexities of peer relationships and group dynamics. By providing opportunities for social interaction, modeling positive social behaviors, and teaching conflict resolution strategies, parents empower children with the interpersonal skills they need to thrive in social settings, both in childhood and beyond.

The importance of emotional intelligence in promoting personal and professional success cannot be overstated. Research has shown that individuals with high levels of EI are more likely to excel in leadership roles, build strong interpersonal relationships, and achieve their goals in both personal and professional domains. Children who possess strong emotional intelligence are better equipped to navigate the challenges of adolescence, make responsible decisions, and build fulfilling careers that align with their values and passions.

Case studies and personal reflections offer compelling evidence of the transformative power of emotional intelligence in children's lives. From the success stories of empathetic leaders who inspire and motivate others to the personal anecdotes of resilient individuals who overcome adversity, these examples underscore the profound impact of emotional intelligence on personal and professional success.

Understanding emotional intelligence in children is essential for fostering social and emotional competence, building strong relationships, and promoting overall well-being. By nurturing self-awareness, self-regulation, empathy, and social skills, parents empower children with the tools they need to navigate life's challenges with resilience, empathy, and confidence. Through intentional support, guidance, and modeling of EI skills, we can cultivate a generation of emotionally intelligent individuals who are equipped to thrive in an increasingly complex and interconnected world.

5.2 Nurturing Emotional Intelligence

Emotional intelligence is a crucial skill set that empowers children to recognize, understand, and manage their own emotions, as well as the emotions of others. It promotes resilience, empathy, and effective communication, laying the groundwork for healthy relationships and successful interactions in various aspects of life. As parents, understanding the importance of nurturing emotional intelligence in our children is essential for their emotional well-being and overall development. Through emotional intelligence activities and empathy-building exercises, we aim to empower parents to cultivate emotional intelligence in their children, promoting self-awareness, empathy, and resilience in their relationships and interactions with others.

One of the most effective strategies for nurturing emotional intelligence in children is to teach emotion recognition skills. Help your child identify and label different emotions, both in themselves and in others. Use books, games, and real-life scenarios to teach them about different emotions and their corresponding facial expressions, body language, and verbal cues. Encourage open communication about feelings and emotions, creating a safe space where your child feels comfortable expressing themselves without fear of judgment or criticism. By teaching emotion recognition skills, parents empower their children to develop self-awareness and empathy, laying the foundation for emotional intelligence and healthy relationship dynamics.

Teaching emotion regulation skills is another essential strategy for nurturing emotional intelligence in children. Help your child understand that all emotions are valid and normal, but that it's essential to regulate their emotional responses appropriately. Teach them coping strategies for managing strong emotions, such as deep breathing, mindfulness, and positive self-talk. Model healthy emotion regulation techniques yourself, demonstrating how to handle stress, frustration, or anger in constructive ways. Provide guidance and support as your child learns to regulate their emotions, offering reassurance and encouragement along the way. By teaching emotion regulation skills, parents empower their children to manage their emotions effectively, promoting resilience and emotional well-being in their daily lives.

Promoting empathy skills is crucial for nurturing emotional intelligence in children. Help your child understand and appreciate the perspectives and feelings of others, encouraging them to show kindness, compassion, and understanding towards others. Model empathetic behavior yourself, demonstrating empathy and compassion in your interactions with others. Encourage your child to take the perspective of others and consider how their words and actions impact those around them. Provide opportunities for your child to practice empathy, such as volunteering or acts of kindness towards others. By promoting empathy skills, parents cultivate a sense of empathy and compassion in their children, fostering emotional intelligence and healthy relationship dynamics.

Creating a supportive and empathetic environment is essential for nurturing emotional intelligence in children. Foster open communication about feelings and emotions, creating a safe space where your child feels comfortable expressing themselves authentically. Listen actively and attentively to your child's thoughts and feelings, validating their experiences and offering support and guidance as needed. Encourage your child to seek support when they are struggling with difficult emotions, reassuring them that it's okay to ask for help when needed. By creating a supportive and empathetic environment, parents foster emotional intelligence and resilience in their children, promoting self-awareness, empathy, and effective communication in their relationships and interactions with others.

Emotional intelligence activities and empathy-building exercises can further reinforce emotional intelligence in children. Engage your child in activities that promote self-awareness, empathy, and emotional regulation, such as journaling, role-playing, or mindfulness exercises. Use storytelling or discussion prompts to explore different emotions and their impact on behavior and relationships. Incorporate empathy-building exercises into your daily routine, such as practicing active listening or role-playing scenarios that require perspective-taking. By incorporating emotional intelligence activities and empathy-building exercises into your child's routine, parents empower them to develop emotional intelligence and resilience, promoting self-awareness, empathy, and effective communication in their relationships and interactions with others.

Nurturing emotional intelligence in children is essential for their emotional well-being and overall development. By teaching emotion recognition, regulation, and empathy skills through modeling, guidance, and practice, parents empower their children to develop self-awareness, empathy, and resilience in their relationships and interactions with others. By creating a supportive and empathetic environment where children feel comfortable expressing their feelings and seeking support when needed, parents foster emotional intelligence and healthy relationship dynamics in their children. Through emotional intelligence activities and empathy-building exercises, parents further reinforce emotional intelligence in their children, promoting self-awareness, empathy, and effective communication in their daily lives.

5.3 Cultivating Self-Awareness

Self-awareness serves as the cornerstone of emotional intelligence, empowering individuals to navigate the intricate landscape of their inner world with clarity, authenticity, and resilience. In the journey of childhood development, fostering self-awareness lays the foundation for emotional well-being, interpersonal competence, and personal growth.

Mindfulness practices offer children a pathway to self-awareness, inviting them to cultivate present-moment awareness and nonjudgmental acceptance of their thoughts, emotions, and sensations. By engaging in mindful breathing, body scans, and sensory awareness exercises, children learn to tune into their inner experiences with curiosity and compassion, cultivating a deeper connection to themselves and the world around them.

Mindfulness practices promote emotional regulation, stress reduction, and mental clarity, empowering children to navigate life's challenges with calmness and resilience.

Journaling serves as a powerful tool for self-expression and self-discovery, providing children with a creative outlet to explore their thoughts, feelings, and experiences. Through journaling prompts, writing exercises, and artistic expression, children can reflect on their inner world, gain insight into their emotions, and identify patterns of thought and behavior. By documenting their thoughts and experiences, children develop a deeper understanding of themselves and their emotions, fostering self-awareness and personal growth.

Self-reflection offers children an opportunity to pause, ponder, and explore their thoughts, feelings, and experiences in a conscious and deliberate manner. Through guided reflection exercises, open-ended questions, and meaningful conversations, children can deepen their understanding of themselves and their emotions, uncovering hidden insights and untapped potential. By encouraging children to reflect on their actions, choices, and values, parents empower them to cultivate self-awareness, integrity, and authenticity in their lives.

The benefits of self-awareness extend far beyond individual well-being, shaping children's relationships, academic achievement, and overall success. Children who possess a strong sense of self-awareness are more likely to exhibit self-confidence, assertiveness, and authenticity in their interactions with others. By understanding their own strengths, weaknesses, and values, children can make informed decisions, set realistic goals, and pursue their passions with purpose and conviction.

Self-awareness also fosters resilience, enabling children to navigate setbacks, challenges, and failures with perseverance. By recognizing their emotions and reactions in difficult situations, children can develop adaptive coping strategies, seek support when needed, and bounce back from adversity with renewed strength and resilience. Self-awareness empowers children to take ownership of their experiences, learn from their mistakes, and grow into confident and resilient individuals who embrace life's challenges as opportunities for growth and learning.

Through guided exercises and self-assessment tools, parents can empower children to deepen their understanding of themselves and their emotions, fostering self-awareness and emotional intelligence. By nurturing the seeds of self-awareness in children, we lay the foundation for a lifetime of self-discovery, personal growth, and well-being. As children develop a deeper understanding of themselves and their emotions, they gain the confidence, resilience, and authenticity to navigate life's challenges with courage, embracing their true selves and fulfilling their potential.

5.4 Developing Self-Regulation

Self-regulation stands as a fundamental skill in a child's journey toward emotional maturity and resilience. It empowers children to navigate the ebb and flow of their emotions and impulses, fostering a sense of control and adaptability in the face of life's challenges.

Relaxation techniques offer children a toolkit for managing stress and regulating their emotions in healthy and adaptive ways. From deep breathing and progressive muscle relaxation to guided imagery and mindfulness exercises, relaxation techniques help children soothe their nervous system, reduce tension, and restore a sense of calm amidst the storms of emotion. By teaching children to recognize the physical signs of stress and practice relaxation techniques, parents empower them to regulate their emotions and responses, fostering emotional stability and well-being.

Stress management skills equip children with the resilience and coping strategies they need to navigate life's challenges with confidence. Through problem-solving exercises, goal-setting activities, and time management techniques, children learn to identify stressors, prioritize tasks, and develop proactive strategies for managing stress effectively. By teaching children to break tasks into manageable steps, seek support when needed, and maintain a positive outlook, parents empower them to overcome obstacles and persevere in the face of adversity.

Cognitive restructuring involves challenging and reframing negative thoughts and beliefs that contribute to emotional distress and maladaptive behaviors. By teaching children to recognize and challenge their irrational thoughts and replace them with more rational and constructive ones, parents empower them to cultivate a resilient mindset and cope with adversity more effectively. Through cognitive restructuring exercises, children learn to reframe setbacks as opportunities for growth, challenge limiting beliefs, and develop a more optimistic and empowered outlook on life.

The importance of self-regulation in promoting emotional stability, impulse control, and resilience cannot be overstated. Children who possess strong self-regulation skills are better equipped to manage their emotions, resist temptations, and make thoughtful decisions that align with their goals and values. By developing self-regulation, children cultivate a sense of agency and autonomy, empowering them to navigate life's challenges with confidence and resilience.

Experiential exercises and real-life examples offer children opportunities to practice and apply their self-regulation skills in a supportive and nurturing environment. From role-playing scenarios and problem-solving activities to mindfulness exercises and relaxation techniques, children learn to regulate their emotions and responses in real-time, building confidence and competence in their ability to cope with life's ups and downs.

Developing self-regulation in children is essential for fostering emotional resilience, impulse control, and adaptive coping skills. By teaching children relaxation techniques, stress management skills, and cognitive restructuring strategies, parents empower them to navigate life's challenges. Through experiential exercises and real-life examples, children learn to regulate their emotions and responses, building the foundation for a lifetime of emotional well-being and success.

5.5 Fostering Empathy and Compassion

Empathy and compassion are the cornerstones of meaningful human connection, fostering understanding, support, and solidarity in the face of adversity. In the journey of childhood development, nurturing these qualities in children is essential for fostering healthy relationships, social connection, and emotional well-being.

Empathy is the ability to understand and share the feelings of others, while compassion is the desire to alleviate their suffering. By teaching children to actively listen to others, validate their feelings, and offer support and comfort, parents empower them to cultivate empathy and compassion in their relationships. Through active listening exercises, children learn to tune into others' emotions, validate their experiences, and respond with empathy and kindness, fostering deeper connections and mutual understanding.

Perspective-taking is another essential skill for fostering empathy and compassion in children, enabling them to see the world through others' eyes and understand their thoughts, feelings, and experiences. By encouraging children to imagine themselves in others' shoes, consider different perspectives, and empathize with their struggles and joys, parents foster empathy and compassion, building bridges of understanding and empathy across diverse backgrounds and experiences.

Acts of kindness offer children tangible opportunities to express empathy and compassion in their daily lives, fostering a culture of caring and generosity in their communities. From simple acts of kindness such as sharing toys and helping a friend in need to larger acts of service such as volunteering in the community or standing up for others, children learn to recognize and respond to the needs of others with empathy and compassion, fostering a sense of belonging and connection.

The benefits of empathy and compassion extend far beyond individual relationships, shaping children's social and emotional well-being and contributing to a more compassionate and inclusive society. Children who possess strong empathy and compassion skills are more likely to form positive relationships, resolve conflicts peacefully, and contribute to a culture of kindness and respect in their communities. By nurturing empathy and compassion in children, parents empower them to become empathetic leaders and agents of positive change in the world.

Empathy-building exercises and empathy training offer children opportunities to practice and strengthen their empathy and compassion skills in a supportive and nurturing environment. From role-playing scenarios and perspective-taking exercises to empathy-building games and storytelling activities, children learn to recognize and respond to the emotions of others with empathy and compassion, building confidence and competence in their ability to foster meaningful connections and support others in times of need.

Fostering empathy and compassion in children is essential for promoting healthy relationships, social connection, and emotional well-being. By teaching children active listening, perspective-taking, and acts of kindness, parents empower them to cultivate empathy and compassion in their interactions with others, building a more compassionate and inclusive society for generations to come. Through empathy-building exercises and empathy training, children learn to recognize and respond to the emotions of others with empathy and compassion, fostering deeper connections and a culture of kindness and respect in their communities.

5.6 Enhancing Social Skills

Social skills serve as the scaffolding upon which children construct their social worlds, fostering meaningful connections, cooperation, and collaboration with others. In the journey of childhood development, nurturing these skills is essential for building and maintaining positive relationships, navigating social situations with confidence, and fostering resilience in the face of interpersonal challenges.

Communication lies at the heart of social skills, enabling children to express themselves clearly, listen actively, and connect with others on a deeper level. By teaching children effective communication strategies such as using "I" statements, active listening, and assertive expression, parents empower them to navigate social interactions with confidence and clarity. Through communication exercises and role-playing scenarios, children learn to communicate their thoughts, feelings, and needs assertively, fostering mutual understanding and respect in their relationships.

Collaboration is another essential skill for enhancing social skills, enabling children to work effectively with others toward common goals and objectives. By teaching children the value of teamwork, cooperation, and compromise, parents empower them to collaborate with peers, family members, and classmates in a respectful and inclusive manner. Through collaborative projects, group activities, and team-building exercises, children learn to leverage their strengths, communicate effectively, and solve problems collaboratively, fostering a sense of camaraderie and achievement in their interactions.

Conflict resolution skills equip children with the tools they need to navigate disagreements, misunderstandings, and conflicts in a constructive and respectful manner. By teaching children active listening, empathy, and problem-solving strategies, parents empower them to resolve conflicts peacefully, assertively, and fairly. Through conflict resolution exercises and role-playing scenarios, children learn to identify underlying needs and interests, generate creative solutions, and negotiate mutually satisfactory outcomes, fostering resilience and conflict resolution skills that serve them well throughout life.

The importance of social skills in promoting teamwork, leadership, and resilience cannot be overstated. Children who possess strong social skills are better equipped to collaborate effectively with others, lead by example, and bounce back from setbacks and challenges in their relationships. By developing social skills, children cultivate a sense of belonging, acceptance, and support in their communities, laying the foundation for positive relationships and success in school, work, and life.

Role-playing scenarios and social skills training offer children opportunities to practice and strengthen their social skills in a supportive and interactive environment. From conflict resolution simulations and group problem-solving activities to communication exercises and leadership challenges, children learn to apply their social skills in real-life situations, building confidence and competence in their ability to navigate social interactions and build satisfying relationships.

Enhancing a child's social skills is essential for fostering positive relationships, teamwork, and resilience in the face of interpersonal challenges. By teaching children effective communication, collaboration, and conflict resolution strategies, parents empower them to navigate social situations with confidence, building stronger connections and a more supportive and inclusive community. Through role-playing scenarios and social skills training, children learn to apply their social skills in real-life situations, building confidence and competence in their ability to build satisfying relationships and succeed in the social world.

5.7 Building a Growth Mindset

A growth mindset stands as a beacon of possibility and resilience, empowering children to embrace challenges, learn from failures, and unleash their full potential through effort and perseverance. In the journey of childhood development, fostering a growth mindset is essential for promoting resilience, motivation, and achievement.

Reframing challenges as opportunities for growth lies at the heart of a growth mindset, enabling children to approach obstacles with curiosity, determination, and resilience. By teaching children to view challenges as stepping stones to mastery, parents empower them to embrace difficulties as opportunities to learn, grow, and improve. Through reframing exercises and growth mindset mantras, children learn to cultivate a positive outlook and mindset that empowers them to tackle challenges with confidence and optimism.

Embracing failure as a learning opportunity is another essential component of a growth mindset, enabling children to recognize that setbacks and mistakes are natural and essential parts of the learning process. By teaching children to see failure as a valuable source of feedback and growth, parents empower them to bounce back from setbacks with resilience and determination. Through failure reflection exercises and growth mindset stories, children learn to embrace failure as a necessary step on the path to success, building resilience and perseverance in the face of adversity.

Seeking feedback to improve is a hallmark of a growth mindset, enabling children to learn from others, set realistic goals, and continuously improve and grow. By teaching children to seek feedback from peers, teachers, and mentors, parents and educators empower them to identify areas for growth and development, set actionable goals, and monitor their progress over time. Through feedback-seeking exercises and growth mindset conversations, children learn to approach feedback with openness and humility, leveraging it as a catalyst for growth and improvement.

The benefits of a growth mindset in promoting resilience, motivation, and achievement are profound and far-reaching. Children who possess a growth mindset are more likely to persevere in the face of challenges, set ambitious goals, and take healthy risks to achieve their dreams. By cultivating a growth mindset, parents empower children to embrace learning as a lifelong journey, unlocking their full potential and achieving success in school, work, and life.

Growth mindset activities and mindset coaching offer children opportunities to practice and strengthen their growth mindset skills in a supportive and nurturing environment. From goal-setting exercises and reflection journals to growth mindset challenges and role-playing scenarios, children learn to cultivate a mindset of growth and possibility, building confidence and competence in their ability to overcome obstacles and achieve their goals.

Building a growth mindset in children is essential for promoting resilience, motivation, and achievement. By reframing challenges as opportunities for growth, embracing failure as a learning opportunity, and seeking feedback to improve, parents empower children to cultivate a mindset of growth and possibility, unlocking their full potential and achieving success in school, work, and life. Through growth mindset activities and mindset coaching, children learn to approach challenges with confidence, optimism, and resilience, building a strong foundation for lifelong learning and achievement.

5.8 Navigating Adversity and Challenges

Life is an unpredictable journey filled with unexpected challenges and setbacks, but it's how we respond to adversity that defines us. As parents, navigating these trials can be both daunting and overwhelming, but fostering resilience within ourselves equips us to weather the storms with strength.

Problem-solving skills stand as pillars of resilience, empowering parents to tackle challenges with a clear mind and a proactive approach. By breaking down problems into manageable steps, brainstorming creative solutions, and taking decisive action, parents can navigate adversity with confidence and effectiveness. Teaching children problem-solving skills from a young age instills resilience, as they learn to approach obstacles with a solution-oriented mindset, fostering independence and resourcefulness in the face of adversity.

Emotional regulation is another essential skill for navigating adversity, enabling parents to manage stress, anxiety, and frustration in healthy and adaptive ways. By practicing mindfulness, deep breathing exercises, and relaxation techniques, parents can soothe their nervous system, reduce tension, and maintain emotional equilibrium amidst life's challenges. Modeling emotional regulation for children teaches them to cope with stress and adversity in constructive ways, fostering resilience and emotional well-being.

Seeking social support serves as a cornerstone of resilience, providing parents with the encouragement, empathy, and guidance they need to navigate adversity with strength and resilience. By reaching out to friends, family members, or support groups, parents can lean on their social network for emotional support, practical assistance, and perspective during difficult times. Building strong social connections not only enhances resilience but also promotes mental health and well-being, as parents feel less isolated and more empowered to face life's challenges.

The importance of resilience in promoting mental health and well-being cannot be overstated. Parents who possess strong resilience skills are better equipped to cope with stress, bounce back from setbacks, and maintain a positive outlook amidst adversity. By cultivating resilience within themselves, parents serve as role models for their children, teaching them invaluable life skills that will serve them well throughout their lives.

Resilience-building exercises offer parents opportunities to strengthen their resilience skills and cultivate a mindset of strength and resilience. From journaling and self-reflection to visualization exercises and gratitude practices, parents can engage in activities that promote resilience and well-being amidst life's challenges. By incorporating these practices into their daily routine, parents can cultivate greater resilience and strength, empowering themselves to navigate adversity with determination.

Navigating adversity and challenges as a parent requires resilience, strength, and perseverance. By honing problem-solving skills, practicing emotional regulation, and seeking social support, parents can navigate life's trials with confidence and effectiveness. Through resilience-building exercises and case studies, parents can cultivate greater resilience within themselves, empowering themselves to weather life's storms with strength and resilience.

5.9 Cultivating Optimism and Positivity

Optimism, with its radiant belief in the promise of better days and the inherent power to effect positive change, serves as a beacon of hope in the face of life's trials. Within the familial sphere, fostering optimism and positivity can imbue every aspect of life with resilience, mental health, and well-being.

Gratitude practices offer a profound pathway to cultivating optimism and positivity within a family. By consciously focusing on the blessings and joys present in everyday life, families can shift their perspective from scarcity to abundance, fostering a deep sense of appreciation and contentment. From keeping gratitude journals and sharing daily gratitude around the dinner table to engaging in acts of kindness and volunteering as a family, gratitude practices cultivate a culture of positivity and abundance, strengthening familial bonds and promoting emotional well-being.

Positive affirmations serve as powerful tools for cultivating optimism and self-belief within a family. By intentionally choosing and repeating positive statements that affirm one's worth, strengths, and potential, family members can reshape their inner dialogue and cultivate a more positive self-image. From creating affirmations boards and reciting positive mantras together to writing affirmations on sticky notes and placing them in visible locations around the home, positive affirmations reinforce a sense of optimism, confidence, and resilience within the family unit.

Reframing negative thoughts is another essential strategy for cultivating optimism and positivity within a family. By challenging and replacing negative thoughts with more constructive and empowering alternatives, family members can cultivate a more optimistic and hopeful outlook on life. From practicing cognitive restructuring techniques and identifying cognitive distortions to engaging in family discussions aimed at reframing challenges as opportunities for growth and learning, reframing negative thoughts fosters resilience, problem-solving skills, and emotional well-being within the family.

The benefits of optimism in promoting resilience, mental health, and well-being within a family are profound and far-reaching. Families who cultivate optimism and positivity are better equipped to navigate life's challenges with resilience and determination. By fostering a culture of optimism, families create a supportive and nurturing environment where members feel empowered to overcome obstacles, pursue their goals, and thrive amidst adversity.

Optimism-building exercises and positivity training offer families opportunities to strengthen their optimism skills and cultivate a more positive outlook on life. From creating vision boards and setting optimistic goals as a family to practicing positive visualization and engaging in optimistic discussions, families can actively cultivate optimism and positivity in their daily lives. By incorporating these practices into their routines and interactions, families can foster a resilient and optimistic mindset that serves as a source of strength and support in the face of life's challenges.

Cultivating optimism and positivity within a family is essential for promoting resilience, mental health, and well-being. By embracing gratitude practices, positive affirmations, and reframing negative thoughts, families can cultivate a culture of optimism that fosters resilience, strengthens relationships, and promotes emotional well-being. Through optimism-building exercises and positivity training, families can harness the transformative power of optimism to overcome challenges, pursue their dreams, and create a brighter, more fulfilling future together.

5.10 Seeking Support and Connection

Parenting is a journey filled with joys, triumphs, and challenges, but no one needs to navigate it alone. In times of adversity, social support and connection serve as lifelines, offering solace, guidance, and strength to weather life's storms.

Reaching out to friends and family stands as a cornerstone of seeking support as a parent. By sharing joys, concerns, and challenges with trusted loved ones, parents can find comfort, empathy, and understanding amidst the ups and downs of parenting. Whether through regular phone calls, coffee dates, or family gatherings, maintaining open lines of communication with friends and family fosters a sense of belonging and support, strengthening familial bonds and promoting emotional well-being.

Joining support groups offers parents opportunities to connect with others who share similar experiences and challenges. Whether it's a parenting group, support group for parents of children with special needs, or online community for new parents, support groups provide a safe space for parents to share their struggles, exchange advice, and offer mutual support. By participating in support groups, parents not only gain valuable insights and coping strategies but also find validation, camaraderie, and a sense of belonging that fosters resilience and well-being.

Seeking professional help when needed is a crucial step in prioritizing mental health and well-being as a parent. Whether it's seeking therapy, counseling, or parenting classes, professional support offers parents the tools and resources they need to navigate challenges, build resilience, and promote healthy family dynamics. By seeking professional help, parents gain access to expert guidance, support, and interventions tailored to their unique needs, fostering emotional healing and growth in the face of adversity.

The benefits of social support in promoting resilience, coping with stress, and maintaining mental health as a parent are profound and far-reaching. Parents who cultivate strong support networks are better equipped to navigate the demands of parenthood. By fostering connections with others, parents create a sense of community and belonging that buffers against the stresses of parenting, promotes emotional well-being, and strengthens family relationships.

Support-seeking and Networking opportunities offer parents practical strategies for cultivating stronger support networks and building more meaningful connections with others. From practicing active listening and empathy in conversations to reaching out to potential support resources in the community, parents can actively seek out and nurture supportive relationships that foster resilience and well-being. By incorporating these practices into their daily lives, parents can cultivate a sense of connectedness and support that enriches their parenting journey and promotes overall well-being.

Seeking support and connection as a parent is essential for promoting resilience, coping with stress, and maintaining mental health. By reaching out to friends and family, joining support groups, and seeking professional help when needed, parents cultivate stronger support networks that buffer against the challenges of parenthood and foster emotional well-being. Through support-seeking and networking opportunities, parents can empower themselves to build more meaningful connections with others, enriching their parenting journey and promoting resilience and well-being for themselves and their families.

5.11 Practicing Self-Care and Well-Being

Parenthood is a journey filled with boundless love, but it can also be demanding, overwhelming, and exhausting. Amidst the myriad responsibilities of raising children, it's easy for parents to neglect their own needs and well-being. However, practicing self-care is essential for promoting emotional well-being and resilience.

Healthy lifestyle habits serve as the foundation of self-care for parents. By prioritizing adequate sleep, nutritious eating, regular exercise, and hydration, parents can nourish their bodies and minds, replenishing their energy reserves and promoting overall well-being. Creating a balanced daily routine that includes time for rest, physical activity, and healthy meals is essential for maintaining physical and mental health amidst the demands of parenthood.

Relaxation techniques offer parents invaluable tools for managing stress and promoting relaxation amidst the chaos of parenting. From deep breathing exercises and progressive muscle relaxation to guided imagery and meditation, relaxation techniques help parents unwind, release tension, and cultivate a sense of calm amidst the whirlwind of daily life. Incorporating brief relaxation breaks into their day, parents can recharge their batteries and approach parenting with renewed energy and clarity.

The importance of self-care in promoting resilience, reducing stress, and preventing burnout cannot be overstated. Parents who prioritize self-care are better equipped to navigate the demands of parenthood with resilience and effectiveness. By taking time to nurture their own well-being, parents not only enhance their own quality of life but also set a positive example for their children, teaching them the importance of self-care and well-being from an early age.

Self-care assessments and well-being workshops offer parents practical tools and resources for prioritizing their own well-being and cultivating greater resilience and strength. From self-assessment quizzes and goal-setting exercises to relaxation techniques and mindfulness practices, parents can explore different aspects of self-care and identify areas where they can make positive changes to enhance their well-being. By participating in well-being workshops, parents can also connect with other parents, share experiences, and support one another in their self-care journey.

Practicing self-care and prioritizing well-being is essential for parents to nurture resilience and emotional well-being amidst the challenges of parenthood. By incorporating healthy lifestyle habits, relaxation techniques, and mindfulness practices into their daily routines, parents can replenish their energy, reduce stress, and cultivate greater resilience in the face of life's challenges. Through self-care assessments and well-being workshops, parents can empower themselves to prioritize their own well-being and create a nurturing environment that supports the whole family's flourishing.

5.12 Embracing Growth and Transformation

Parenthood is a transformative journey, marked by moments of joy, challenges, and profound growth. In the quest to raise happy, healthy children, parents embark on a journey of self-discovery and personal growth, cultivating emotional intelligence and resilience along the way. The importance of embracing growth and transformation as a parent cannot be overstated, and how personal growth contributes to resilience, well-being, and fulfillment. Through reflection exercises and personal growth challenges, parents are empowered to embrace their journey of growth and transformation, fostering greater emotional intelligence and resilience in their lives and within their families.

Embracing growth and transformation as a parent begins with a willingness to embrace vulnerability and uncertainty, and to view challenges as opportunities for learning and growth. Parenthood is filled with moments of uncertainty, from navigating sleepless nights to facing unexpected parenting challenges. By reframing these moments as opportunities for growth, parents can cultivate resilience and adaptability, fostering a mindset of continuous learning and improvement.

Self-discovery is an essential aspect of the parenting journey, enabling parents to gain insight into their values, strengths, and areas for growth. Through self-reflection exercises and journaling, parents can explore their beliefs, emotions, and experiences, gaining clarity and self-awareness. By understanding themselves more deeply, parents can cultivate greater emotional intelligence, empathy, and resilience, enhancing their ability to navigate the complexities of parenthood with authenticity.

Personal growth challenges offer parents opportunities to step outside their comfort zones, take healthy risks, and expand their horizons. Whether it's pursuing a new hobby, learning a new skill, or challenging limiting beliefs, personal growth challenges encourage parents to stretch themselves and embrace change. By pushing past fears and limitations, parents cultivate resilience, confidence, and a sense of empowerment, strengthening their capacity to face life's challenges with courage and resilience.

The journey of growth and transformation as a parent is not always easy, but it is profoundly rewarding. As parents navigate the highs and lows of parenthood, they discover new depths of strength, resilience, and love within themselves. By embracing their journey of growth and transformation, parents not only foster their own well-being and fulfillment but also model valuable life skills for their children, teaching them the importance of resilience, self-discovery, and continuous growth.

Reflection exercises offer parents opportunities to pause, reflect, and gain insight into their experiences and emotions as parents. By setting aside time for quiet reflection, parents can gain clarity and perspective, deepening their understanding of themselves and their parenting journey. Through guided reflection prompts and journaling exercises, parents can explore their values, goals, and aspirations, gaining insight into their priorities and areas for growth.

Personal growth challenges encourage parents to step outside their comfort zones and pursue new experiences and opportunities for growth. Whether it's committing to daily self-care practices, setting boundaries, or pursuing a long-held dream, personal growth challenges empower parents to take action and create positive change in their lives. By embracing challenges and pushing past limitations, parents cultivate resilience, confidence, and a sense of empowerment, enhancing their well-being and fulfillment as individuals and as parents.

Embracing growth and transformation as a parent is essential for fostering emotional intelligence and resilience in the journey of parenthood. By embracing vulnerability, self-discovery, and personal growth challenges, parents cultivate resilience, adaptability, and a sense of empowerment, enhancing their well-being and fulfillment in the process. Through reflection exercises and personal growth challenges, parents can deepen their understanding of themselves and their parenting journey, fostering greater emotional intelligence and resilience within themselves and within their families.

Chapter 6: Establishing Routines and Boundaries with Love and Consistency

Routines and boundaries are essential for promoting well-being and resilience in children by providing structure, support, and guidance for navigating life's challenges. By promoting self-care, coping skills, and positive coping mechanisms within routines and boundaries, parents empower their children to prioritize their own well-being and develop the resilience and inner strength needed to thrive in today's complex world. Moreover, by encouraging children to seek support and practice self-compassion during times of adversity, parents foster a sense of connectedness and belonging that promotes resilience and well-being throughout their lives.

6.1 The Importance of Routines

Routines serve as the scaffolding of daily life, offering structure, predictability, and stability to individuals of all ages. From infants to adults, routines play a crucial role in promoting a sense of security, organization, and self-regulation. In the context of parenting, establishing routines for children holds immense importance, contributing to their overall well-being and laying the foundation for success in various aspects of life.

One of the primary benefits of routines for children is the sense of security they provide. Consistent daily routines create a predictable environment in which children know what to expect, reducing anxiety and uncertainty. From regular mealtimes and bedtime routines to consistent morning and evening rituals, routines offer children a sense of stability and safety, enhancing their overall sense of well-being and security. Additionally, routines promote organization and self-regulation in children. By establishing regular schedules and expectations, parents help children develop important time-management skills and self-discipline. Through consistent routines, children learn to prioritize tasks, manage their time effectively, and regulate their behavior, laying the groundwork for success both in school and in life. Moreover, routines provide children with a sense of autonomy and control over their environment, empowering them to make choices and take ownership of their actions.

Furthermore, routines have a profound impact on various aspects of children's health and development. Consistent bedtime routines, for example, are associated with improved sleep quality and duration, leading to better cognitive function, mood regulation, and overall well-being. Similarly, regular mealtime routines promote healthy eating habits and nutritional intake, reducing the risk of childhood obesity and other health problems. Research has shown that children who follow consistent study routines at home tend to perform better academically, demonstrating higher levels of concentration, motivation, and academic achievement.

Beyond the immediate benefits for children, establishing routines also benefits parents by reducing stress and enhancing family functioning. Predictable routines streamline daily activities, making it easier for parents to manage their time and responsibilities. By establishing clear expectations and routines, parents can minimize power struggles and conflicts with their children, fostering a more harmonious and cooperative family environment. Routines provide parents with opportunities for quality bonding time with their children, whether it's reading bedtime stories, sharing family meals, or engaging in shared activities.

The importance of parents setting routines for their children cannot be overstated. Routines provide children with a sense of security, organization, and self-regulation, promoting their overall well-being and success in various aspects of life. From better sleep and nutrition to improved academic performance and family functioning, the benefits of routines for children are manifold. By establishing consistent daily routines, parents create a stable and supportive environment in which children can thrive and reach their full potential. Through research findings and personal experiences, it's evident that routines play a vital role in laying the foundation for a happy, healthy, and successful childhood.

6.2 Understanding Boundaries

In the intricate tapestry of human relationships, boundaries serve as the threads that weave together respect, trust, and mutual understanding. For children, understanding and establishing boundaries are vital aspects of their social and emotional development, shaping the way they interact with others and navigate the world around them.

Boundaries are the guidelines, rules, or limits that define acceptable behavior and interactions in relationships. For children, boundaries provide a framework for understanding social norms, expectations, and personal autonomy. From a young age, children learn about boundaries through their interactions with caregivers, peers, and the world around them. Whether it's respecting personal space, expressing emotions appropriately, or understanding consent, boundaries play a crucial role in shaping children's social and emotional development.

Physical boundaries encompass the space and touch boundaries that children establish with others. Teaching children to respect personal space and boundaries helps them develop an understanding of consent, bodily autonomy, and respect for others' physical boundaries. Whether it's asking permission before hugging a friend or respecting a sibling's personal belongings, children learn to navigate physical boundaries in their interactions with others, fostering mutual respect and trust.

Emotional boundaries relate to children's ability to recognize, express, and regulate their emotions in healthy ways. By teaching children to identify and communicate their feelings effectively, parents empower them to set emotional boundaries and assert their needs and preferences in relationships. Whether it's expressing discomfort with teasing or setting limits on emotional demands, children learn to establish emotional boundaries that protect their well-being and foster healthy relationships.

Relational boundaries encompass the expectations and limits that children establish within their relationships with others. From setting limits on screen time and social media use to defining expectations for behavior and communication, children learn to negotiate relational boundaries that reflect their values, preferences, and personal integrity. By establishing clear boundaries in their relationships, children cultivate a sense of self-respect and assertiveness, fostering healthier and more fulfilling connections with others.

The consequences of boundary violations can be profound, affecting children's emotional well-being, self-esteem, and relationships. When children's boundaries are disregarded or violated, they may experience feelings of powerlessness, resentment, and distrust. Over time, repeated boundary violations can erode children's sense of self-worth and undermine their ability to establish healthy relationships based on mutual respect and trust.

Through case studies and real-life examples, we can understand the pivotal role of boundaries in children's relationships. For instance, a child who consistently sets boundaries with peers regarding personal space and belongings fosters a sense of self-respect and assertiveness. In contrast, a child who struggles to assert their boundaries may find themselves in situations where their needs are disregarded or dismissed, leading to feelings of frustration and resentment.

Setting boundaries for children is essential for fostering healthy relationships, maintaining personal autonomy, and promoting emotional well-being. Whether it's physical, emotional, or relational boundaries, children learn to navigate the complexities of relationships and assert their needs and preferences with confidence and respect. By teaching children about boundaries and modeling healthy boundary-setting behaviors, parents empower them to navigate the world around them with integrity, self-respect, and resilience. Through understanding and respecting boundaries, children lay the groundwork for fulfilling relationships built on trust, respect, and mutual understanding.

6.3 Establishing Routines with Love

In the dynamic landscape of family life, routines serve as essential pillars, providing structure, predictability, and stability for children as they navigate the world. However, the manner in which routines are introduced and maintained can significantly impact a child's well-being and sense of security. Establishing routines with love involves creating a nurturing and supportive environment where routines are introduced and upheld with care, compassion, and understanding.

At the heart of establishing routines with love lies the recognition that children thrive in environments characterized by warmth, understanding, and empathy. When introducing routines, it's essential for parents to set realistic expectations that take into account the unique needs, abilities, and temperament of their child. By acknowledging the individuality of each child and tailoring routines to suit their developmental stage and preferences, parents create a sense of ownership and empowerment that fosters cooperation and compliance.

Positive reinforcement plays a crucial role in reinforcing desired behaviors and motivating children to adhere to routines. Whether through verbal praise, encouragement, or rewards, parents can provide positive feedback to acknowledge their child's efforts and achievements in following routines. By focusing on the positive aspects of behavior rather than dwelling on mistakes or shortcomings, parents create a supportive and affirming atmosphere that encourages children to embrace routines willingly and enthusiastically.

Modeling desired behaviors is another effective strategy for establishing routines with love. Children learn by observing and imitating the actions of their parents and caregivers, so it's important for parents to demonstrate the behaviors and habits they wish to instill in their children. Whether it's maintaining a regular bedtime routine, practicing good hygiene habits, or engaging in regular family meals, parents serve as powerful role models whose actions speak louder than words.

Empathy, patience, and flexibility are essential qualities for parents to cultivate as they navigate the ups and downs of establishing routines with love. Empathy allows parents to understand and validate their child's feelings and perspectives, fostering a sense of connection and trust. Patience enables parents to remain calm and composed in the face of resistance or setbacks, recognizing that change takes time and consistency. Flexibility allows parents to adapt routines to accommodate unforeseen circumstances or changes in their child's needs, ensuring that routines remain relevant and effective over time.

Practical tips and parenting techniques offer readers actionable strategies for establishing routines with love in their own homes. For example, creating visual schedules or charts can help children understand and anticipate daily routines, fostering a sense of predictability and security. Using gentle reminders and prompts can help children transition between activities smoothly and minimize resistance. Additionally, involving children in the process of establishing routines by soliciting their input and preferences can increase their sense of ownership and investment in following routines.

Establishing routines for a child with love involves creating a nurturing and supportive environment where routines are introduced and maintained with care, compassion, and understanding. By setting realistic expectations, providing positive reinforcement, and modeling desired behaviors, parents can foster cooperation and compliance while promoting harmony and well-being in their homes. Through empathy, patience, and flexibility, parents can adapt routines to meet the diverse needs of their children and create a sense of security and stability that lays the foundation for healthy development and success.

6.4 Setting Boundaries with Love

In the intricate dance of family relationships, boundaries serve as essential markers, delineating the limits of acceptable behavior, communication, and interaction. Setting boundaries with love involves communicating expectations, values, and limits in a manner that upholds the dignity and autonomy of every family member.

At the heart of setting boundaries with love lies the principle of clear communication. Parents must clearly articulate their expectations, values, and limits to their children, ensuring that there is no ambiguity or misunderstanding. By openly discussing boundaries and the reasons behind them, parents create a shared understanding and mutual respect within the family. Parents should actively listen to their children's thoughts, feelings, and concerns, validating their perspectives and fostering open communication channels.

Empathy is a cornerstone of setting boundaries with love, as it allows parents to understand and acknowledge their child's emotions and experiences. By empathizing with their child's perspective, parents demonstrate respect for their child's autonomy and individuality, fostering a sense of trust and connection. Parents should strive to empathize with their child's feelings and needs, even when setting boundaries or enforcing consequences, demonstrating that their actions are rooted in love and concern.

Consistency, firmness, and follow-through are essential elements of setting boundaries effectively. Parents must enforce boundaries consistently and fairly, without wavering or making exceptions based on circumstance. By maintaining firm but loving boundaries, parents establish a sense of predictability and security for their children, helping them understand the consequences of their actions and choices. Additionally, parents must follow through on consequences when boundaries are violated, demonstrating that there are real and meaningful consequences for behavior.

Compassion and understanding play a vital role in addressing boundary violations with love. When children cross boundaries, parents should respond with empathy and understanding, seeking to understand the underlying reasons for their behavior. By addressing the root cause of boundary violations, parents can help their children learn from their mistakes and make better choices in the future. Moreover, parents should avoid using punitive or shaming tactics when addressing boundary violations, instead focusing on teaching and guiding their children towards more appropriate behavior.

Role-playing scenarios and conflict resolution exercises offer practical tools for parents to practice setting and maintaining boundaries with love. By simulating real-life situations and exploring different approaches to setting boundaries, parents can develop their communication and problem-solving skills, empowering them to navigate challenging situations with confidence and compassion. Moreover, conflict resolution exercises teach children valuable skills for resolving conflicts and disagreements in a respectful and constructive manner.

Setting boundaries for a child with love involves communicating expectations, values, and limits in a manner that respects their dignity and autonomy. By employing strategies such as clear communication, active listening, empathy, consistency, firmness, and follow-through, parents can establish healthy boundaries that promote respect, trust, and mutual understanding within the family. Through compassion and understanding, parents can address boundary violations with love, guiding their children towards responsible and respectful behavior. Role-playing scenarios and conflict resolution exercises offer practical tools for parents to practice setting boundaries effectively and empower their children to navigate relationships with respect and empathy.

6.5 Promoting Flexibility and Adaptability

In the ever-changing landscape of family life, promoting flexibility and adaptability is essential for navigating the twists and turns that arise on the journey. While consistency provides stability and predictability, embracing flexibility and adaptability allows individuals and families to respond effectively to the evolving needs and circumstances of daily life.

In the context of family life, promoting flexibility and adaptability begins with recognizing and embracing the inherent unpredictability of daily life. While routines and boundaries provide structure and guidance, they must also be flexible enough to accommodate the changing needs and circumstances of individuals and families. Parents can promote flexibility by encouraging problem-solving skills and teaching children how to adapt to unexpected changes or challenges.

Problem-solving skills are essential for promoting flexibility and adaptability in children. By teaching children how to identify problems, brainstorm solutions, and evaluate alternatives, parents empower them to navigate challenges and setbacks with confidence and resilience. Problem-solving skills foster a proactive mindset, encouraging children to view obstacles as opportunities for growth and learning rather than insurmountable barriers.

Compromise and negotiation are also valuable tools for promoting flexibility within family dynamics. By encouraging open communication and collaboration, parents empower children to express their needs and preferences while also considering the perspectives of others. Compromise and negotiation teach children valuable skills for resolving conflicts and finding mutually acceptable solutions, fostering empathy, cooperation, and teamwork.

Flexibility fosters resilience by teaching children how to adapt to change and bounce back from setbacks with determination. In today's rapidly changing world, resilience is a critical life skill that enables children to navigate challenges, overcome obstacles, and thrive in the face of adversity. By promoting flexibility and adaptability, parents equip their children with the tools and mindset they need to navigate life's ups and downs with confidence and resilience.

Furthermore, flexibility encourages creativity and innovation by fostering an open-minded and adaptive approach to problem-solving. When children are encouraged to explore new ideas, experiment with different approaches, and embrace uncertainty, they develop the confidence and creativity to think outside the box and find innovative solutions to complex problems. Flexibility nurtures a sense of curiosity and exploration, inspiring children to approach challenges with curiosity, enthusiasm, and a willingness to take healthy risks.

However, promoting flexibility and adaptability also presents challenges, particularly in striking a balance between structure and spontaneity. While routines and boundaries provide stability and predictability, excessive rigidity can stifle creativity and inhibit growth. Conversely, too much flexibility can lead to chaos and inconsistency, undermining the sense of security and stability that routines provide.

Promoting flexibility and adaptability in children is essential for nurturing resilience, creativity, and innovation in family dynamics. By teaching problem-solving skills, encouraging compromise and negotiation, and fostering a mindset of curiosity and exploration, parents empower their children to navigate life's challenges with confidence and resilience. While consistency provides stability and predictability, flexibility allows children to adapt to change and uncertainty with confidence.

6.6 Navigating Transitions and Changes

Life is a journey marked by transitions and changes, each presenting new opportunities for growth, learning, and transformation. Whether it's starting school, moving to a new home, or welcoming a new sibling, transitions are inevitable in a child's life, requiring them to adjust their routines and boundaries accordingly. Navigating these transitions with resilience is essential for helping children thrive in the face of change.

Effective communication is key to helping children navigate transitions and changes. Parents should be open and honest with their children about upcoming changes, providing age-appropriate information and addressing any concerns or questions they may have. By fostering open communication channels, parents create a supportive and trusting environment where children feel comfortable expressing their thoughts and feelings about the transition.

Preparation is another essential strategy for helping children navigate transitions successfully. Parents can prepare their children for upcoming changes by providing them with information, resources, and support to help them understand and cope with the transition. This may include visiting new schools or neighborhoods, discussing changes in routines and schedules, and involving children in decision-making processes whenever possible.

Self-care is equally important for both children and parents during times of transition. Transition periods can be stressful and overwhelming, so it's essential for parents to prioritize their own well-being and model healthy coping strategies for their children. By taking time to engage in self-care activities such as exercise, relaxation techniques, and hobbies, parents can reduce stress and maintain a sense of balance and perspective amidst change.

Flexibility and adaptability are essential qualities for navigating transitions. Children who are able to adapt to change and embrace new experiences with an open mind are better equipped to navigate transitions successfully. Parents can foster flexibility and adaptability in their children by encouraging them to approach change with curiosity, optimism, and a willingness to learn and grow.

Support and community play a vital role in providing stability and reassurance during times of transition. Whether it's seeking support from family, friends, or community organizations, having a strong support network can help children and parents feel more confident and capable of navigating transitions successfully. By surrounding themselves with caring and supportive individuals, families can weather the challenges of transition with greater resilience and optimism.

Resilience-building exercises and self-reflection offer valuable tools for empowering children to navigate transitions with confidence and optimism. By practicing resilience-building activities such as problem-solving skills, positive thinking, and gratitude exercises, children can develop the inner strength and resilience they need to navigate change. Self-reflection encourages children to explore their thoughts, feelings, and reactions to transitions, helping them gain insight into their own coping strategies and resilience-building skills.

Navigating a child's transitions and changes requires patience, understanding, and resilience. By fostering open communication, providing preparation and support, and prioritizing self-care, parents can help their children navigate transitions successfully. Through flexibility, adaptability, and support from their community, children can develop the resilience and optimism they need to embrace change with confidence. By empowering children with resilience-building exercises and self-reflection, parents can help them navigate transitions with confidence, optimism, and a sense of resilience.

6.7 Cultivating Self-Regulation and Responsibility

In the journey of childhood development, the cultivation of self-regulation and responsibility is vital for fostering independence, resilience, and success. Routines and boundaries serve as powerful tools in this endeavor, providing structure and guidance for behavior and decision-making.

Routines and boundaries serve as the scaffolding upon which self-regulation and responsibility are built. By establishing clear expectations, limits, and consequences, parents provide children with a framework for understanding appropriate behavior and making responsible decisions. Routines provide structure and predictability, helping children develop self-discipline and time-management skills. Boundaries delineate the limits of acceptable behavior and provide guidance for navigating social interactions and decision-making.

Goal-setting is a powerful strategy for cultivating self-regulation and responsibility in children. By helping children set realistic and achievable goals, parents empower them to take ownership of their actions and work towards meaningful objectives. Whether it's academic goals, behavioral goals, or personal goals, goal-setting teaches children the importance of planning, perseverance, and self-discipline in achieving success.

Self-monitoring is another essential skill for cultivating self-regulation and responsibility. Parents can encourage children to reflect on their thoughts, feelings, and actions, helping them develop self-awareness and self-control. Self-monitoring involves paying attention to one's behavior and its consequences, identifying areas for improvement, and making adjustments as needed. By fostering self-monitoring skills, parents empower children to take responsibility for their actions and make informed decisions.

Accountability is a key component of cultivating self-regulation and responsibility in children. Parents should hold their children accountable for their actions and decisions, providing feedback and guidance when necessary. Accountability teaches children the importance of taking ownership of their behavior and facing the consequences of their actions. By holding children accountable in a fair and consistent manner, parents help them develop a sense of responsibility and integrity.

Fostering autonomy and independence is essential for promoting self-regulation and responsibility in children and adolescents. Parents should encourage their children to make age-appropriate decisions, solve problems independently, and take initiative in pursuing their goals. By giving children opportunities to make choices and learn from their experiences, parents empower them to become self-reliant and confident individuals.

Positive reinforcement is a powerful motivator for promoting responsible behavior in children. Parents should praise and reward their children for demonstrating self-regulation, responsibility, and other positive behaviors. By acknowledging and celebrating their achievements, parents reinforce desired behaviors and encourage children to continue making responsible choices.

Natural consequences are also important for promoting responsible behavior in children. When children make poor choices or fail to meet expectations, parents should allow them to experience the natural consequences of their actions. Natural consequences help children understand the link between their behavior and its outcomes, fostering accountability and promoting learning and growth.

Character education and values clarification exercises offer valuable tools for empowering children to cultivate self-regulation and responsibility. By teaching children about virtues such as honesty, integrity, and perseverance, parents instill a strong moral compass that guides their behavior and decision-making. Values clarification exercises help children identify their core values and understand the importance of aligning their actions with their beliefs.

Cultivating self-regulation and responsibility in children is essential for fostering independence, resilience, and success. Routines and boundaries provide the structure and guidance needed to develop self-discipline and decision-making skills. By employing strategies such as goal-setting, self-monitoring, and accountability, parents empower their children to take ownership of their behavior and make responsible choices. Fostering autonomy, providing positive reinforcement, and allowing for natural consequences further promote responsible behavior. Through character education and values clarification exercises, parents empower children to cultivate self-regulation and responsibility, laying the foundation for a lifetime of success and fulfillment.

6.8 Building Healthy Relationships and Communication

Routines and boundaries are not just about structure and discipline; they also serve as the foundation for healthy relationships and effective communication within families.

Routines and boundaries provide a sense of predictability and stability in family life, creating an environment where trust can flourish. When children know what to expect and understand the rules and expectations, they feel secure and confident in their relationships with their parents and siblings. Routines also establish a framework for communication, providing regular opportunities for family members to connect and interact with one another.

Boundaries are essential for establishing respect and maintaining healthy relationships within families. When boundaries are clear and consistently enforced, family members learn to respect each other's space, belongings, and feelings. Boundaries also help prevent conflicts and misunderstandings by delineating acceptable behavior and communication patterns.

Effective communication is vital for building and maintaining healthy relationships within families. Parents should model positive communication skills, such as active listening, empathy, and assertiveness, to help children learn how to express themselves effectively and respectfully.

Assertiveness is another important communication skill for children to develop, as it allows them to express their thoughts, feelings, and needs in a clear and respectful manner. Children should learn how to assert themselves confidently and assertively, without being aggressive or passive-aggressive. Assertiveness empowers children to stand up for themselves and communicate their boundaries effectively.

Relationship-building exercises offer valuable opportunities for families to strengthen their bonds and foster trust and respect. Activities such as family meetings, shared hobbies, and collaborative projects encourage family members to connect and communicate with one another in meaningful ways. By spending quality time together and engaging in activities that promote cooperation and teamwork, families can build strong and resilient relationships that withstand the test of time.

Communication skills training provides children with the tools and strategies they need to communicate effectively and respectfully with others. Parents can teach their children how to express themselves clearly and confidently, listen actively and empathetically, and resolve conflicts peacefully and constructively. By equipping children with these essential communication skills, parents empower them to build healthy relationships and navigate the complexities of social interactions with confidence and ease.

Routines and boundaries play a crucial role in establishing healthy relationships and communication patterns within families. By providing structure and stability, routines and boundaries create an environment where trust, respect, and mutual understanding can flourish. Through effective communication strategies such as active listening, assertiveness, and conflict resolution, families can cultivate healthy relationships and foster open, honest, and supportive communication with one another. By engaging in relationship-building exercises and communication skills training, families empower their children to build strong and resilient relationships that enrich their lives and bring them closer together.

6.9 Fostering a Sense of Security and Belonging

In the ever-changing landscape of family and community life, routines and boundaries serve as the bedrock upon which a sense of security and belonging is built.

Routines and boundaries provide a sense of security and stability in our lives, creating a predictable environment where children feel safe and supported. When children know what to expect and understand the rules and expectations, they feel more secure and confident in their surroundings. Routines also help children develop a sense of mastery and competence, as they learn to navigate their daily lives with ease and confidence.

Rituals and traditions are powerful tools for fostering a sense of belonging and identity within families and communities. Whether it's celebrating holidays, birthdays, or cultural traditions, rituals provide opportunities for families to come together and connect with one another. Rituals create a sense of continuity and belonging, helping children develop a strong sense of their cultural heritage and identity.

Shared values are another important aspect of fostering a sense of belonging and connection within families and communities. When families share common values such as honesty, respect, and compassion, they create a cohesive and supportive environment where everyone feels valued and respected. Shared values provide a moral compass that guides behavior and decision-making, fostering a sense of unity and solidarity within the family and community.

Inclusivity and diversity are essential for promoting a sense of belonging and connection within families and communities. When families embrace diversity and celebrate differences, they create a welcoming and inclusive environment where everyone feels valued and accepted. By exposing children to different cultures, perspectives, and experiences, parents broaden their children's understanding of the world and promote empathy, tolerance, and acceptance.

Community-building activities provide opportunities for families to connect with one another and build relationships with their neighbors and community members. Whether it's participating in community events, volunteering for local causes, or joining community organizations, families can contribute to the fabric of their community and foster a sense of belonging and connection.

Relationship-building exercises offer valuable tools for fostering connection and communication within families. By engaging in activities such as family dinners, game nights, or storytelling sessions, families can strengthen their bonds and create lasting memories together. These activities provide opportunities for families to connect on a deeper level and build trust and intimacy.

Fostering a sense of security and belonging in children requires a combination of routines, boundaries, rituals, traditions, shared values, inclusivity, and community connection. By providing a stable and predictable environment, parents create a sense of safety and support that allows children to thrive. By celebrating diversity and embracing inclusivity, parents promote acceptance and understanding, fostering a sense of belonging and connection within families and communities. Through community-building activities and relationship-building exercises, parents empower their children to build strong and meaningful relationships that enrich their lives and contribute to the well-being of their communities.